MW01286529

PRAISE FOR GIVE ME A YEAR

"*Give Me a Year* is Shonda in book form: authentic, bold, and full of joy. Through her 12 New Things® challenge, she invites us to step outside our comfort zones, embrace change, and trust in the journey—knowing that growth, faith, and fun can (and should) go hand in hand. Shonda doesn't just talk about transformation—she lives it, leading with courage and conviction, always guided by her belief that faith and action create miracles.

If you're ready to shake up your routine and start living life with more adventure, purpose, and laughter, this book is your perfect guide. Grab a copy, try something new, and let Shonda be the friend who inspires you every step of the way."

—MICHAEL PHILLIP LEVINE, transformational life coach, speaker, author, and former Hollywood agent

"In a world that celebrates overnight success, Shonda Scott's *Give Me a Year* reveals a more powerful truth: Transformation happens through consistent, intentional steps taken day after day. What distinguishes this work is its profound accessibility. Scott doesn't deal with abstract ideals but with the tangible reality of small victories that create momentum for breakthroughs. Her vulnerability becomes our courage; her methods become our framework for possibility. Scott's innovative approach deeply inspires me as someone dedicated to creating pathways where none existed for our young leaders and encouraging them to step outside their comfort zones.

For dreamers of any age standing at the threshold of their potential, this book whispers a revolutionary truth: You need only commit to taking the next right step with purpose and presence. The journey awaits. The time is now."

—CRISTINA MANCINI,
author and CEO of Black Girls Code

"Shonda moves through the world with a kind of *joie de vivre*, never failing to appreciate the beauty and wonder all around us—whether it's around the world or around the corner. Her debut book, *Give Me a Year*, provides a glimpse into her joyful journey and invites readers to come along for the ride. Buckle up, embrace new things, and live a full life!"

—MAYA L HARRIS, lawyer, policy advocate, and writer

GIVE ME A YEAR

12 NEW THINGS TO EMBRACE
CHANGE AND LIVE YOUR BEST LIFE

GIVE ME A YEAR

SHONDA SCOTT

WONDERWELL
PRESS

This publication is designed to provide accurate and authoritative information in regard to the subject matter covered. It is sold with the understanding that the publisher and author are not engaged in rendering legal, accounting, or other professional services. Nothing herein shall create an attorney-client relationship, and nothing herein shall constitute legal advice or a solicitation to offer legal advice. If legal advice or other expert assistance is required, the services of a competent professional should be sought.

Published by Wonderwell Press
Austin, Texas
www.gbgpress.com

Copyright © 2025 Shonda Scott Enterprises Worldwide, Inc.

All rights reserved.

Thank you for purchasing an authorized edition of this book and for complying with copyright law. No part of this book may be reproduced, stored in a retrieval system, or transmitted by any means, electronic, mechanical, photocopying, recording, or otherwise, without written permission from the copyright holder.

This work is being published under the *Wonderwell Press* imprint by an exclusive arrangement with *Wonderwell*. *Wonderwell*, *Wonderwell Press*, and the *Wonderwell logos* are wholly-owned trademarks of *Wonderwell*.

Distributed by Greenleaf Book Group

For ordering information or special discounts for bulk purchases, please contact Greenleaf Book Group at PO Box 91869, Austin, TX 78709, 512.891.6100.

Design and composition by Greenleaf Book Group
Cover design by Greenleaf Book Group
Cover images used under license from ©Adobestock.com

Publisher's Cataloging-in-Publication data is available.

Print ISBN: 978-1-963827-27-9

eBook ISBN: 978-1-963827-28-6

To offset the number of trees consumed in the printing of our books, Greenleaf donates a portion of the proceeds from each printing to the Arbor Day Foundation. Greenleaf Book Group has replaced over 50,000 trees since 2007.

Printed in the United States of America on acid-free paper

25 26 27 28 29 30 31 32   10 9 8 7 6 5 4 3 2 1

First Edition

IN GRATITUDE

Gratitude is the key that unlocks our blessings. It is paramount to me to show gratitude in all things.

First, giving honor to God, who is the head of my life, giving me the fortitude, courage, and ability to share my authentic life experiences in the following pages. I am grateful to God for co-creating my gift of life with my parents, Arthur Bishop and Frazier Marie.

I dedicate this book to my son, Austin. From the moment that God blessed me with you, my life was forever changed for the better. You were the New Thing that elevated my world and molded me as a person. You are a true blessing, and I am grateful to be your mom.

In loving memory of my ancestors and grandparents:

Paris-Monroe (Grandpa Scott),
Elizabeth (Grandma Scott),
Robert Daniel (Granddaddy),
and Frazier Vonne (Grandmother).

CONTENTS

PREFACE

The 12 New Things© Lifestyle grew out of a period of much-needed change for me. To the outside world, I was a seemingly well-rounded, happy individual. I had achieved success in business as an innovator, fourth-generation entrepreneur, strategic thinker, and writer. I was what many considered to be an accomplished woman. But inside, I felt something was missing: I lacked true fulfillment and joy in some areas of my life. I began looking for inspiration in books and from peers and professionals but didn't find solutions to fill the void. I had come to a place in life where I needed more; my son was now an independent, thriving adult, and I had more free time to explore as a single, self-aware woman. I didn't have all the answers, but I knew I needed to dig deeper, to get out of my not-quite-fulfilling routine, and start mixing it up.

With my reality check in hand, I decided to try something new. Not something earth-shattering and over the top, just a small thing to break my cycle. My "New Thing" was to start taking the more scenic route to work, even though it would make my commute longer. With that, I started listening to inspirational audiobooks instead of the same old talking heads on news radio. This led to noticing and appreciating the things in my city I'd simply driven right past before. This small New Thing gave me inspiration to do more New Things. I eventually committed myself to doing something new and different each month.

As part of my birthday celebrations in 2019, I created the 12 New Things campaign, challenging myself to do something I'd never done before each month for a year, pushing myself to consistently embrace change in ways I discovered were both positive and a lot of fun. 12 New Things has now become a way of life, facilitating an evolution and a renewal in me.

Then the COVID-19 pandemic hit. Everything shifted overnight, and that really magnified the importance of a 12 New Things Lifestyle: We all had to adjust to new ways of doing old things. Normal everyday activities, once done in person, were now done remotely. But that also meant that classes, meetings, seminars, church services, and all sorts of activities became more widely accessible to everyone without leaving home. Businesses began to innovate. Restaurants, grocery stores, and pharmacies designed services to bring orders to your car for "contactless" pickup.

Trying New Things became essential to stay viable.

Many businesses were able to find new and creative ways to continue, expand, and flourish. In contrast, others, unable to change and pivot swiftly enough, sadly faded from existence. I took a page out of the former's book and used the opportunity of being sheltered in place for so long to become more creative with my New Things activities.

That was the beginning.

As I began sharing my experiences with others, I came to the realization that it was motivating them to seek out their own New Things. From there, I created the 12 New Things concept and website (12newthings.com), where others could join me on this journey of novelty and growth. What started as one small New Thing for me grew into a lifestyle, which grew into a movement, which has reintroduced me to others as a motivational speaker and coach. Now, I'm here to be your best thought-partner.

I hope you will come on board the 12 New Things Lifestyle, too.

INTRODUCTION

The Power of 12

There is power and spiritual significance in the number 12.

There are 12 months in a year.

The number 12 is connected to bringing about God's kingdom. God specified that 12 unleavened cakes of bread be placed every week in the temple with frankincense. Abraham produced 12 tribes. Jesus Christ recruited 12 men as his disciples.

The number 12 has been associated with the completion of a full cycle and moving to new beginnings in harmony as your life shifts in a positive direction, and that's why I chose it for the 12 New Things Lifestyle.

What Is the 12 New Things Lifestyle?

The 12 New Things Lifestyle is about doing new and different things to move you out of your comfort zone with harmony. It's a lifestyle choice that starts with the challenge to do just one New Thing each month for a year. Once you open yourself to new adventures and activities, New Things you aren't necessarily looking for or can't even imagine will reveal themselves, expanding your world and creating more significant opportunities in your life. Doing things you've never done before helps to disrupt your cycle. Continuing in set patterns can feel safe and comfortable, but the reality is you can't grow if you just do the same old things over and over again.

I believe in the wisdom of the saying, "Be the change that you wish to see in the world." This quote by Mahatma Gandhi points to a key fact of change: It begins from within. But many of us have a deep-rooted tendency to put others first. In doing so, we neglect our relationship with our self. Therefore, we forget that our job is to love ourselves, or maybe we've never learned to love ourselves in the first place. Whatever your reason for not prioritizing yourself, I'm here to tell you it is time for a paradigm shift. You deserve and are within reach of true, sustainable happiness. Allow me to guide you to a kinder, gentler way of treating the most important person in your life: *you*. Throughout these pages I will share how change and doing different things have opened doors to new and brighter paths throughout my life, and I'll help you do the same.

How Does It Work?

Unlike New Year's resolutions, which, let's be honest, are often hard to stick to or finish, the 12 New Things Lifestyle is a straightforward, doable approach you can easily integrate into your life in big or small ways. As opposed to many other self-help books that make extraordinary demands or set unrealistic stipulations, my guidelines to change will increase your enjoyment and success without requiring total reinvention.

By adopting my 12 New Things Lifestyle, you will soon grow mentally, physically, and spiritually. Anyone can do it, whether they're eighteen or eighty years old. All it requires is welcoming change and concretely articulating what that change can look like in your own life—one step at a time, one month at a time.

Fellow joy seekers, it's time to start making moves, beginning with a dozen new challenges spread out over the year to launch your 12 New Things Lifestyle. So, where do we start?

Getting Started

Beginning is simple. All it takes is to make a commitment to yourself to embrace change and complete your first New Thing. If you start with one small New Thing, I'm confident once you set your mind to that, you will be well on your way to doing at least one New Thing a month. Before you know it, a year will have passed, and you will be on your way to living a 12 New Things Lifestyle.

Since tracking your growth is key to visualizing your 12 New Things journey, begin by selecting a nice journal or using the 12 New Things journal to inspire your daily review. Reflection is important to your growth, so make time to write in the journal as part of your morning routine. For your first entry, reflect on where you are in your life at this moment. How are you feeling, not just health-wise but in your spirit? How does your soul feel? Be as honest and authentic as possible.

Next, let your mind wander; think about the things you have daydreamed about but have yet to make time to do. Make a list of those things, no matter how big or small, near or far. Is it a car ride or a plane trip away? Does it require you to have a particular skill or tool? Is it something that includes someone else, or even a group, to accompany you? Or is it some part of your everyday? As you take a look around, you may be surprised by how easily you can come up with one New Thing to pursue in every aspect of your daily life. Whatever it is, no matter how major or minor, write it all down.

As you read through the chapters where I recount some of my personal journeys, you may find something in my adventures spurs your memories of things you've wanted to experience. Embrace those memories and outside inspirations. Spend some time with your list, keep revisiting it, and know that change is a moving target.

For now, look at your list and choose a small New Thing you have been thinking about. On a new page, write a list of the steps necessary to do that New Thing (your goal).

Each day, review the steps and plan to do something that will move you toward your new goal. Track your progress; check things off as you complete them. It's amazing how accomplished you'll feel just from the process of checking off daily goals. It is essential to keep in mind that what you're doing today is building toward your future; what you are experiencing today is based on what you did yesterday (in the past). Keeping track of this in your journal will also help you see if you're on the way to that New Thing. Another benefit to reviewing your journal each day is that it can alert you when your path is not aligned with your goal, so you can consider what steps you need to take to get back on track.

As you embark on your New Thing, continue to journal about what you are doing and what you are discovering about yourself and the world around you. Remember to note any challenges you face, the hurdles you overcome, and the outcomes you achieve. Keep in mind that as we become busy with work, family, and life, we often place our dreams on the back burner. This is why it is crucial to stay consistent and have tools like your checklist and your journal to keep you on track.

In the following chapters, you will read about how the 12 New Things Lifestyle has manifested in my life. We will explore some of my 12 New Things adventures and some personal experiences that have helped me to evolve and excel. Your journey will no doubt look very different from mine, but the themes we talk about, using my adventures as examples, will strengthen your mindset and help you forward on your path. Each chapter addresses a different theme, and you can read them in order or not—growth is seldom linear, but always rewarding.

The goal throughout is to help you to embark on your own journey. Remember the most important part of the 12 New Things journey is *you*—it is all based on your decision to embrace change, overcome fears, and develop ways to expand to live your best life.

Now, let's jump right in!

EXERCISES:

Once you have your journal, begin documenting your journey:

1. Write down your dreams of what you really want to do, the changes you want to see in your life now or perhaps in the next five years, places you would like to visit, and things you've put off or put to the side.

2. Write a list of New Things you have never done.

3. Pick your first New Thing. Research, plan, and create your checklist to achieving it. (Remember, your first New Thing doesn't have to be big.)

4. Do the New Thing!

5. Reflect in your journal about how it feels to do or pursue your first New Thing.

6. Go back to your list of dreams and things you've never done but want to do. Select your next New Thing.

   - Calendar one New Thing for each month of the coming year. If you do not have 12 New Things to start or can't decide right now, no need to worry. Once you begin your 12 New Things journey, inspiration and self-knowing will find you along the way.

   - Note the steps you will need to take for each New Thing.

7. Consider sharing your New Things journey with someone else. Sharing your experiences and growth will help not only you but also others who are (or perhaps need to be) on this journey as well.

"We change our world when we change us."

—Gandhi

1

JUMP RIGHT IN

Sometimes as we follow a path in life, we come to a crossroad that presents us with opportunities and options along the way. The choice is either to move past our fears and accept the challenge or take the more comfortable route. Later in life when those opportunities reemerge, it could be a sign that it's time to reconsider and take advantage of the missed experience. "Jump right in" is my way of taking the sting out of procrastination and mindless worry over trivial things. Thinking this way in certain situations is powerful—it can help us get started without delay. However, it's crucial to remember that jumping in without prior thought or planning can be detrimental in business, money matters, or any activity that we are not qualified to undertake, potentially leading to harmful, impulsive actions and consequences.

On my twenty-first birthday anniversary (which is what I've taken to calling every birthday after my twenty-first), I chose to fly to Honolulu. This city has felt like a second home to me ever since my high school years and holds a special place in my heart. Visiting the Hawaiian Islands always gives me a sense of peace because I know I can relax there, especially by the pristine waters of Waikiki Beach. I mean, who couldn't?

This flight was not just a journey to the island, but a pilgrimage for my 12 New Things solo birthday trip.

Since I had decided that on this trip I would do something new and different, on the flight I struck up a conversation with my seatmate, Naoko, a Japanese American woman with a soft voice. During our conversation, we discovered that we'd both attended college at the University of California, Los Angeles, though not at the same time. Naoko and I chatted amicably the way alumnae often do until, at one point in our conversation, I brought up that my only regret about college was that I never swam on the legendary UCLA Bruins swim team.

It's true; I started swimming at age two, took lessons until I was about seven, then spent several years pleading with my parents to let me join a local swim team in Oakland, my hometown. Finally, they gave in and found a team they thought would be a good fit for me. To my surprise, I was the only African American girl on the swim team until I eventually recruited one of my African American friends, Rachelle, to join. Even though I knew that, historically, the sport of swimming was exclusionary, and many African Americans didn't know how to swim or didn't enjoy the sport, I was still surprised that I was the only Black girl on my swim team. I loved to swim. I couldn't imagine life without water and just thought everyone else felt this way too.

Then, around my sophomore year of high school, I had to choose between swimming and my other passion, basketball, because, as my pediatrician, Dr. Jenkins, used to say, "Swimming is like a jealous mistress." It insists on sucking up all your attention and commitment. If you were to look around for two-sport athletes, you'd be hard-pressed to find a swimmer among them, simply because it's too demanding of a sport. So, I ultimately opted to play basketball, not least because it did not require the high level of hair management that swimming demanded. Joking aside, this meant that I had decided to end my career as a competitive swimmer and give up on my dream to become the first Black female to swim on the U.S. Olympic team.

"Funny you should bring that up," Naoko said. "I actually did swim on the UCLA team."

"Oh, my goodness," I said like a fangirl, beyond thrilled to meet someone who had lived one of my wildest dreams. "That's such a fantasy for me. I love that. I swim now, but I do it as my workout." I told Naoko about how I'd started swimming again after my cousin Shannan passed away from breast cancer at age twenty-nine. I wanted to do something to honor her memory and raise money for cancer research, and since running is not my thing, I looked for alternatives. By chance, I learned about an event called Swim for Women with Cancer. As soon as I got back in the water training for this event, I realized how much I still loved to swim, even if I didn't love the intensive training regimen required to do it competitively. My passion for swimming had never gone away.

Naoko told me about an open swim event she did called Swim Across America, which raises money for pediatric cancer research and treatments. "You should do the open swim this year, Shonda. You need to keep up your training in the swimming pool, but then you also need to do some open swim training to be ready to swim in the ocean."

I thought, *Okay, that seems doable*, even though I thought I had given up swimming in cold water when my swim team days ended. But why not? This would be something new. Plus, I knew I'd be wearing a wetsuit for warmth. When I'd previously swum for a cause, I'd been able to see the few obstacles that had presented themselves as simply a part of the challenge for me to overcome. My cousin had gone through a far more difficult ordeal with cancer—I could do something as simple as trying to figure out how to swim in cold water. That was the mindset I used to psych myself up for the event.

I had fantasized in the past about open swimming in the ocean, but I hadn't gone through with it because the "you are putting your life at risk" language in the paperwork turned me away. It was time I overcame that fear!

I had to remember that the water is a spiritual place for me and always has been. I often have what you might call "devotional moments" when I'm doing my training in the water, as I swim for a cause. On my own in the water with no distractions, just me, the Lord, and the chuff-chuffing sound of my arms and legs moving me along.

When I landed back home from my birthday trip, I went straight online, clicked on the links Naoko had sent me, and signed up as a participant on her team for the open swim. I told myself I'd start training in March, in the bay on the East Bay side, which runs south from Oakland to San Jose. Funny, when you hear the word "bay," most people think of a warmer, calmer alternative to the ocean. After all, a bay is by definition a protected area, so it seemed logical that the chilly, relentless waves of the northern Pacific Ocean would dissipate and lose a good part of their chill by the time the water reached the relative safety of the bay.

I'm not sure these were the exact thoughts coursing through my head a few weeks later as I dove into the water for my first open swim. It's hard to recall anything going through my mind at the time because my head, hands, and feet were instantly FROZEN! I was in and out of that so-called bay faster than you can say, "*I am not doing this!*" And guess what? That's exactly what I said, italics included, as I leapt back onto shore.

That might have been the end of the whole thing, except that I'm not a quitter. Never have been. Try as I might, I simply couldn't leave things undone and just walk away. I decided to turn to what always gets me through challenges: prayer! I began praying to God to make sure this open swim was something the Lord had ordained. I had to make sure God was with me. The last thing I wanted to do was jump in the deep blue sea without God with me blessing my path. I could already see how dangerous going out in those rough waters would be, and I thought, *Let me make sure I'm not doing this on my own.* I heard God speak to me in a quick, clear, and unequivocal manner. "Shonda! You got this, and I am here," He said in a soft voice like Naoko's. I had a feeling He would say that, but you know, it never hurts to check. All kidding aside, it was important for me to feel I would be in the warm embrace of my faith, especially when faced with a challenge as daunting and icy cold as this one.

The next time I returned to the bay, I ventured out for real. I brought along my production crew, cameras and all, to record this 12 New Things moment because I wanted to document the excitement and journey of the swim challenge. That's a big part of what each of these 12 New Things is about for me. My aim is to have fun by stepping out of my comfort zone and sharing my experiences with others, though thus far, the fun part of this challenge had yet to reveal itself to me.

I slipped into the icy cold water slowly and swam for a few quick minutes. When I came back ashore, I told my film director, "Ramasses, you know what? Next time I'll do more. Or not. If I do it, fine. If I don't, at this point, at least I got in the ocean and swam."

I began reasoning with myself because this was not getting any easier, and all I'd managed to do at this point was equivocate. The whole time I'd been in the water, I was afraid of hyperventilating from the cold. I kept telling myself, *You cannot just quit or make up some excuse to justify quitting.* When I got home, I sat down and began researching "how to stay warm in the water." My research quickly revealed I was going about it all wrong. For starters, taking my time getting into the water made it worse. The correct method is to jump right in and immediately start swimming. I also learned that I'd been breathing incorrectly. I thought my breathing was too heavy and labored, which made it feel like I was hyperventilating and thus causing me to panic, but the article I read said my breathing was correct: "Your breath is what keeps you warm." I also learned about thermal caps, gloves, booties, and the time-honored technique of putting Vaseline on areas of your body where heat escapes. Isn't it funny how a little knowledge goes such a long way?

Armed with my new thermal tricks and tools, I was able to swim farther out on my next try, going even longer than I'd anticipated. Only this time, I couldn't seem to swim straight because the current kept pushing me off course. One stroke forward, two strokes back. I was beginning to feel like this New Thing I'd chosen, like a bad date, came with a host of unpleasant quirks I couldn't see coming until it was too late.

Over time I became aware that whether we like it or not, any New Thing that challenges us to step out of our comfort zone arrives with a bunch of unknowns in its wake. It's precisely that fear of the unknown that often holds us back from making a change in our lives for the better.

That is why I encourage you to build an element of fun into whatever you choose for your 12 New Things. By doing this, you'll guarantee that even if things don't work out the way you hope, you'll at least have had fun trying. And if things do work out, as they most likely will, you'll end up with a win-win.

Equally important to the 12 New Things ethos is the idea that failure is okay. That's no misprint: Failure is sometimes an excellent option. Let me explain what I mean before you assume I've lost my mind. Everything we've learned to do in our lives is the result of our having failed at it, at least at first. No babies come out of the womb speaking eloquently, eating properly, or knowing how to make good choices in life. Instead, they babble, create unspeakable messes with their food, and stumble into danger with reckless abandon. And then something miraculous happens. They begin to learn. I mean, why did I expect to handle the open water swim with the natural ease of a dolphin just because I knew how to swim in a pool? Why did I expect that I'd have a perfect open-ocean swim on the first try? Instead, I had to learn to give myself grace and be okay with failing (at first) so I could learn how to develop my skills and swim correctly in these new circumstances.

Meanwhile, back in San Francisco Bay, the water wasn't getting any warmer, nor the waves and currents any weaker. The only thing that had changed was my mental attitude toward the challenge that lay before me. I was humbled, and that was all right with me because I refused to let my determination diminish simply because the circumstances were tougher. I became more immersed in the spiritual part of being out in the ocean and how I felt when I was in the water. I began to focus on the other inspiring stimuli available, like the birds flying over me and the sound of the waves' motion.

You may find as you venture into new waters (pun intended) and start to build your confidence that external factors can cause you to second-guess yourself. For me, once I completed a few more practice swims and was feeling pretty good, suddenly everybody I knew and loved became concerned about what I was doing. My aunt, my doctor, you name it.

"Oh, my God. You're swimming in the bay?" my aunt called to say.

"Aren't there sharks in that water?" asked an old friend.

"The bay? Seriously, Shonda?" said my doctor.

"Look, I've already started. I'm doing the swim," I explained confidently to each concerned party.

Confidently, that is, until I happened upon an article about sharks. *Yikes! Really God, is this your idea of a joke?* Fortunately, I soon found a way to rationalize it . . . the article was about sharks in Florida and, therefore, not an indication of . . . Oh, never mind. I decided to hold out hope that California sharks were vegan, or pescatarian, at least. I did a total of four practice ocean swims, each time going a bit farther out before swimming back, until I was confident. Even during my travel for work, I kept my swim workouts going to stay in shape. I also started weight training to build additional muscle strength. I was as ready as I could be. So, time for my big moment, right? Shonda completes the swim in record time, her friends and relatives wonder how they could have ever doubted her, and even the sharks rejoice. What a wonderful world this could and would be!

Except when it's not. A week before the scheduled swim, I called the event organizers. I asked for clearance to have my upcoming triumph-over-adversity filmed. That's when I learned I'd somehow missed the memo about how we had to swim the entirety of the nearly two-mile route, from point A to point B. *Wait, what?* For some reason, perhaps because it would have scared the stuffing out of me had I known the truth, I'd naively assumed that the start and finish lines were one and the same, that we'd be swimming a loop.

"Oh, no," the man on the phone helpfully explained. "You go in one place, and you get out at another, so you have to do the whole route. This is not an event for beginners."

When I hung up, I could practically feel my fear of sharks dropping to the number two position on my current list of anxieties, ceding its place to an acute and overwhelming fear of drowning. And on video, no less (the man gave the okay for my cameraman to be there, perhaps to deliver the eulogy).

I knew a bit about drowning from an incident I'd had in middle school. My family often went to the beach in Santa Cruz, California, where the waves were extremely strong, but you could still go in and play in the shallows. One time I went in, and a wave hit me dead on. I tried to swim up to the surface, but I found I couldn't. It was as though the wave had grabbed me by the ankle and was pulling me straight down. I was drowning. I immediately started freaking out. But my swimming instincts kicked in and told me to stop fighting, and to my surprise, I popped up to the surface. As I pulled myself back onto the beach, coughing, I looked out, realizing no one had even seen what happened. The whole thing occurred in a matter of seconds, and my parents were totally unaware.

Less than three minutes. That's how fast a person can drown. So, imagine how quickly you could go under out in the deep water of the bay. Fortunately, the same guy on the phone emailed me a while later saying that I could have a "swim angel," meaning someone who had participated in the swim before could come along and act as my spotter. *Okay, I thought, that means I'm less likely to drown, but still, how on God's green earth was I going to make it all that way?* It was too late to turn back: I'd put too much effort into my preparations. I mean, I'd posted about it on Instagram, so I had to go through with it. Plus, I'd done so well at vanquishing each of the obstacles that had presented themselves to that point, and as I said earlier, quitting was not part of my DNA.

Ring ring . . .

"Hello?"

"Hi, Naoko? It's Shonda. I heard you agreed to be my angel?"

It's true. Naoko had immediately agreed to be my swim angel, though I suspected this would be her first time ever doing it because I could clearly hear a tinge of uncertainty in her voice. Still, I was beyond grateful. Everything was in place, and I was ready.

About a week before my swim, my grandmother became ill. I was worried and pondered, if she left us, would I still want to swim? She passed a day before the event, and I realized that my swim really was an act of faith and part of a spiritual journey. I felt as if God had given me a swim angel and a heavenly angel to help me get through. I felt that my grandmother would want me to exercise my faith rather than sit in mourning. So, I got the courage to continue with the swim.

My grandmother, Mrs. Frazier Thomas-Scurry, lived her entire life in Houston, Texas. She was a nurse and a deaconess in the church. She was 103 and 348 days old when she passed. Grandmother was the true matriarch of our family; strong-willed and loving. She was a devoted servant of the Lord; it was her faith in the Lord Jesus Christ that was the foundation of my belief. She was a fashionista and traveler as well. Even when my grandfather was alive (he lived to age ninety-three), she would travel all across America and the Caribbean with her friends and children.

Her celebration of life service was held on what would have been her 104th birthday at the megachurch in Houston, Texas, which she and my grandfather had helped grow and where she served in leadership for over eighty years. It was packed. I was so grateful for President Biden and Vice President Harris, who sent written recognitions and regards from the White House, and Congresswoman Sheila Jackson Lee of Houston, Texas, who provided an in-person tribute in honor of my grandmother's memory, a life well-lived. My grandmother was a force of nature and woman of deep faith. It was her spirit I would need to channel to get me through the turbulent ocean waters during my swim.

The day before Swim Across America, I checked in at The Ritz-Carlton in San Francisco. It would only be a quick trip from there to the swim starting point. Fridays are my "me day," so I decided to treat myself to the hotel stay, and I knew it would allow me to relax and prepare better for the early swim.

Since we were filming, we arrived early Saturday morning. Once the camera crew got set up, I checked in. That's when I learned from the event organizer that I would be swimming alongside a rockstar team of all Olympians. Such a pleasant surprise!

Once we had all the equipment on, all 200 swimmers ran across the beach, jumped in the ocean, and began swimming. Although the day was calm, I felt every wave. It started to feel as if the water was pulling my legs down again. In my mind, I began to feel concerned, especially when I thought about how far out in the ocean we were, with no shore nearby: just the massive body of water surrounding me. Part of me wanted to melt into the ocean and just rest. Thank God for my swim angel, Naoko. Swim angels stay with you the entire swim, and Naoko coached me the whole way. She rose to the challenge, deftly switching between being an angel and a drill instructor when I needed one in the moment. Just what I needed to snap out of it and stay focused on finishing the swim. I was impressed with her strength and focus. As a lifeguard, I know how intense and stressful being responsible for someone's safety in the water can be.

Naoko refused to let me give up, even when I felt my body being compromised by anxiety. "No, keep going," she'd say over and over, knowing from experience that debilitating fatigue would creep up on me if I gave it a chance. I remember being in the water surrounded by boats, canoes, and San Francisco Police Department officers on Jet Skis. I felt safe in that regard, but it was still a huge ocean with no bounds. I swam past places I'd visited and imagined swimming by (like Alcatraz, the Golden Gate Bridge, Ghirardelli Square, and Fort Mason). As for the path, my swim angel and the safety canoe rider alongside us kept me on the proper route and out of the other way of the current. If we entered into the wrong current, we could be swept away along with any hope of finishing the race in the allotted time. So much to think about in addition to fighting the fatigue in my body.

At the midway point in my ocean swim

Whenever I hinted at giving up or asked about going onto the boat, Naoko simply shouted encouragement. "No, just kick, Shonda! Just kick!" I could feel myself longing for the days when I was a little girl and my mom would buy me a Nestle Drumstick ice cream cone if I did well in swim lessons. That blissful memory kept me going, along with Naoko's steadfast refusal to let me quit. Everyone needs an angel like this to encourage them through the rough patches in life. It felt metaphoric.

An hour later, the event was officially over—although I'd already walked out of the water sometime before, because not only had I swum the entire route, but I'd also completed it in less than forty-five minutes!

Emerging from the ocean with my swim angel, Naoko

As I neared the finish line, I was flushed with emotions and broke down in the water, crying. I thought about the incredible accomplishment and what it took to finish the swim. I thought about all those I was swimming for who'd fought or were fighting cancer, and I thought about my grandmother. My swim team members had to guide me to the mat at the finish as the announcer shouted words of encouragement to ensure I crossed the official finish.

When I came out of the water, the first face I saw was my son's; then I became aware of my family and friends, all cheering me on. They were all really excited for me and very impressed. I was impressed with myself too. I remember one of my teammates, a male Olympian, asked me at the end, "How was it? How was your first swim?" My response: "It was GREAT, and I am never doing that again." We all shared a laugh together. This one of my 12 New Things is a one-and-done.

Our team: Olympians and honorary Olympians

Swimming with this team of Olympians was a dream come true. And, oh, my goodness, they were all amazing and so supportive. The captain actually came over and hugged me before we officially met. It was the sweetest thing. I later found out she felt it in her spirit that I needed a hug. I didn't realize it, but it all made sense to her when she found out about my grandmother. Her seeing that in my face was truly Divine intervention. She, too, was swimming in memory of a loved one, her husband. Nevertheless, everyone was so full of positive energy, and getting to swim as a member of this team—as an "honorary Olympian," as my mother put it—was beyond anything I'd ever imagined.

After the event, my mother and I stayed at the hotel to relax, decompress, and reflect on the amazing day, which we closed with a lovely dinner and a Champagne toast. This adventure allowed me to indulge in a longtime dream that was hidden deep within my heart and my past, which as an adult I didn't believe would ever come to fruition. Just jumping in to try this New Thing opened me up to believing that New Things can come from past dreams that you thought you had left far behind.

EXERCISES:

1. Write a list of sports or other activities you did in the past or have thought about learning but never tried. Note why you stopped each activity or why you never started.

2. Select one of those activities to do. What steps would you have to take to begin doing that activity in a new way or for the first time? What would you need to do to take that activity to the next level and move you out of your comfort zone?

"Then you will see and be radiant,
And your heart will thrill and rejoice;
Because the abundance of the sea will be turned to you,
The wealth of the nations will come to you."
—Isaiah 60:5

2

SOUL PROPRIETORSHIP

Referring to "soul," Jesus says, "It is the seat of
your memory, your feelings, your imagination,
convictions, desires, and your affections."

—Mark 8:35-37

The Hebrew word (nephesh) translates soul to a
living, breathing conscious body.

—Encyclopedia of Judaism

In today's hustle culture, how do we find balance between being career-driven and caring for and feeding our inner soul? Becoming an entrepreneur helped me come to the realization that any change or rebalance I wanted in my life or business had to start with me. This is a universal principle. Ironically, changing aspects of oneself or one's life is a scary thing for most people. Be it changing your routine, career, or job, people often find this sort of change very difficult because they link their self-identity to these things. Therefore, change in these areas often causes disruption and anxiety.

Yet, it is the understanding that change is a constant in our lives that brings peace. As the title of the song says, "Everything Must Change." Therefore, change isn't something to fear, but rather something to embrace as an opportunity to learn, grow, and try more New Things.

From birth, we are instinctively open to change and new learning. It's a necessary part of life that enables us to survive and grow. As long as you live, you should never stop learning and expanding your horizons. With each New Thing we experience or encounter, we learn to feed our soul, making us more confident and open to seeking more. Growing, learning, and evolving are paramount to becoming the person you see in your dreams. Personally, I continue to strive to do New Things to improve and strengthen my mind, body, and business.

Each of us can find a New Thing related to career, business, or even personal development that will help to change our direction or enhance where we are, especially when we feel we are not in the place we want to be. Most people average forty-plus hours of work weekly, meaning work takes up the majority of one's waking hours. To survive, many become stuck in a job or business situation that no longer serves them.

Or are faced with that person at the company just oozing with a toxic aura that affects everyone. The workplace can become so consuming that even our off-hours get eaten up by thoughts of the workday. It's similar to having a love-hate relationship with a boyfriend or girlfriend. Life-draining relationships can numb your mind if you allow them to. This is where change comes in to save the day and help you pivot. Incremental changes in ourselves can begin to have a significant impact on our lives. Making these changes allows you to begin to open yourself up to a new situation.

I have had to make changes many times in my life and career. I was raised seeing my parents run their business, and I am a fourth-generation entrepreneur. The first entrepreneur on my father's side that we can trace was my great-grandfather William Pitts. Grandpa Pitts was born to an enslaved Black woman and a White slave owner in 1864. He became a real estate developer, building homes for Black families in the segregated area of Lincoln Hills in Golden, Colorado, in the 1920s. Our family still owns the cabin he built for the family in 1926; it is now a historic landmark. Business is in my DNA, and my own entrepreneurial streak has been showing itself since I sold cookies for the Girl Scouts.

When I first started out after graduating from UCLA, I was the director of concessions for my family's airport concessions business in a major international airport. I loved the work but soon found myself itching to create my own business. I wanted to make my way in the world without my parents' support. It was as if, deep inside, I had something to prove to myself and those around me. At that time, I was engaged, and my fiancé was working for a corporation that had him based in Las Vegas while I worked and lived in the Bay Area. After a year, we had both grown tired of the long-distance part of our relationship. We wanted to be together in the same city, or at least the same state! Since my situation was more flexible and I was ready to relocate, I decided to move to Las Vegas.

When I moved to Las Vegas, I didn't know anyone except my fiancé. Since I was on the path to live on my own before getting married, I decided to get my own place instead of moving in with him. I rented an apartment and immediately started working on my business venture in Las Vegas, putting together a proposal for my own airport concessions deal at the Las Vegas Airport. I poured my heart and soul into this proposal, using everything I had learned from working with my parents to prepare the documents for the package, then submitted it.

While I waited through the lengthy approval process, I accepted a job as a manager for my favorite shop in the Forum Shops at Caesars Palace. I enjoyed the work, met some amazing people who became lifelong friends, and got a 40 percent discount on clothes. At times, it seemed as though I were living in the Land of Oz. The Forum Shops area was so Las Vegas; they had people who actually walked around dressed as Antony and Cleopatra. It was a real job! And a highly coveted one, no less. Caesars had recruiters from the mall come into the store one day and ask me if I was interested in being Cleopatra. I was flattered, yes, only because they had to think you were beautiful to play Cleopatra. But I said no—one, because I could not imagine explaining to my folks back in Oakland that I had a job strutting around the mall as Cleopatra, and two, because I heard those headpieces were heavy. The last thing I needed was neck problems from walking around with that huge headpiece on all day.

After a few months of living in Las Vegas, life changed again! My fiancé's company relocated him back to California. At the same time, my airport concessions proposal had moved up to the short list of the top four best submittals. By this time, my fiancé and I were having problems, so I made the decision to stay in Las Vegas and start my new life, and he went back to California. Good thing I had my own apartment, so when he left, I didn't have to move. I was good!

Then, the day came for my interview for the concession. I left the boutique to go in front of this panel of suits. Of course, none of them looked like me. So, there I was, all by myself. They asked me detailed questions about my proposal, inquiring about who formulated the numbers for the financial projections, who wrote the proposal, who developed the marketing plan. They asked who came up with everything. I wasn't prepared for any of this, but I tried to answer with confidence. The only answer I had was "me"—I'd put together the whole thing.

I look back and think about how young and naive I was then. Now, after over twenty years in business, I realize the value and importance of a team. Back then, I was on a mission to prove that I could do it all by myself. Thank God I answered that wake-up call and have since surrounded myself with an excellent team of brilliant, innovative people who are my true thought-partners and co-executors.

The other issue the panel of suits had with my proposal was their misconception that my business was not local. They believed that because my family had concessions in California, I was somehow connected to their business. And that was the last thing Las Vegas wanted, a California corporation coming in and "taking" their business. Needless to say, I didn't win the project.

I was thrilled to be considered; it was a huge learning experience for a young businesswoman just starting out. There really wasn't anything wrong with the proposal I submitted. In fact, they actually used my idea to begin putting coffee concessions in the airport. When I proposed this concept, there weren't any coffee concessions in any airports. Some say I was ahead of my time. Today, when my team is going after a proposal, we identify the best person for each role. We prepare for weeks, working on the proposal, practicing the presentation, praying, and going in to win the work. We are a small but mighty force. But this is now. Back then, I had just broken up with my fiancé after moving to a new city and leaving my family, and my proposal for my dream project had just been turned down. I was devastated.

Not only did I see my professional dreams deferred, but the dreams of getting married and owning my own business were also gone. Or were they? It was time to take a trip—a long, faraway trip—to clear my head, heal my wounds, release stress, and figure out my next move. At this point, I'm contemplating staying in Vegas or maybe doing another New Thing. So, I started to daydream.

I'd always loved the idea of moving to an island and living the island life. This dream came from when my family and I often traveled to St. Thomas in the U.S. Virgin Islands, maybe a couple of times a year. On one trip, I met a group of people from New York and California. They were my age and had decided to move to St. Thomas. I was so impressed with their decision to live and work in this paradise. That was something I always wanted to do but could never figure out when to do it. What better time than now?

As I planned the trip to reevaluate my life while enjoying the beach in St. Thomas, I found myself thinking maybe I'd open a coffeehouse or business there. I envisioned myself living there, having fun in paradise, and hanging out with my friends. I immediately arranged for a week to check out places to live and meet up with my friends.

Once I landed in St. Thomas, I checked into the hotel and set out to explore the island. I reached out to my East Coast friends I'd met there in years past, hoping to make some quick connections. This was before the internet and smartphones, so communication was limited. Unfortunately, I soon learned all my friends had moved back to the mainland. I quickly realized how small the island was when locals I did not know knew where I was staying and began calling the hotel and leaving messages for me. This made me very uncomfortable as a woman alone on an island. I didn't want to live alone in a place that small.

Now what? I was sad because my fun friends, whom I romanticized about having this big adventure with, were gone. Well, I was already there, so I decided to make the best of the trip, take time to relax on the beach, pray, and reflect on what I needed to do next.

As I lay on the beach and prayed, God gave me a whole vision for my next move; he told me to stay in Vegas and bring St. Thomas there. The guidance and vision were as clear as the pristine ocean water. I envisioned using the plans I had presented to the airport to design my own business with a Caribbean twist. The concept was to bring a slice of paradise and culture to Sin City.

And at that moment, I birthed the Java Hut, the first Black woman-owned gourmet coffeehouse and the first cybercafé in Las Vegas. I found a wonderful location in a strip mall between a grocery store and an adorable used bookshop owned by a lovely local family. The bookstore owners were elated when they heard I was moving in next door; they thought it was the perfect complement to their business. And it was.

I took my sadness and immersed myself in my business. The theme and décor were "Welcome to Paradise." We had a mocha java shake before the Frappuccino. It had ice cream, chocolate, and espresso blended, topped with whipped cream and a chocolate-covered espresso bean. We had open mic poetry and comedy nights, political forums with local elected officials, murder mystery dinners, and catered special events. We hired students from local high schools and quickly became part of the community. The location was on the route from a densely populated residential area to the famous Las Vegas Strip, so we benefitted from the foot traffic of the dancers, entertainers, professionals, and students commuting back and forth.

We had loads of fun at the Java Hut, leaving me with fond memories of a city where I started out not knowing anybody, and became a young leader in the community. Some people thought my business was a franchise chain; others thought I had some high-paid "sugar daddy" who let me play at running a coffee shop (it was Las Vegas, after all). But neither was true. The Java Hut was a blessing sent straight from God to help me pivot during a time of enormous change in my life. I wanted to create something different from my parents' business, which I did on my own. It was a significant component of how I found myself.

Then, a few years later, my life changed again. I found myself not feeling well, throwing up for days to the point where I thought I was going to die. One night, I found myself face up, looking at the vaulted ceilings in the luxury townhouse I had built in Vegas. I loved my place because I picked out everything in it! It was my first solo real estate purchase, and I was proud of myself for it. But I was just not feeling like myself. Looking up, I prayed to God to help me understand what was happening. In a quiet voice, God whispered, "You are pregnant, and it is a boy." I'm both perplexed and amazed at the same time because I could not recall ever hearing God's voice speak to me in this fashion. Then, God repeated it just as quietly and clearly. It was confirmed: I was going to be a mom. I decided the best course of action would be to give birth in Oakland near my family and my doctors, then come back to Vegas after I'd had the baby.

Naive, young, and looking for a lifeline, I entrusted all my business accounts to an attorney who was supposed to set up a restructuring of my business to allow me time to breathe, not think about business, and have my son. Unfortunately, a few months after giving birth, I received a notice that the attorney hadn't filed any of the paperwork. He'd taken the money and done nothing of what he was hired to do. At that point, I had to find the best attorney in California to help me dissolve the business and file a full-on bankruptcy, Chapter 7. I lost my assets, my property, everything—and I had to literally start over. So, I did.

Over the years, I began to rebuild my life step-by-step and reimagine myself. I found a new direction and a new career, putting me on a new path to where I am today. Everything I had lost, I regained tenfold. From the ashes of that past bankruptcy, I have since dusted myself off and am now blessed to own a multimillion-dollar business enterprise with awesome teams of employees, multiple revenue streams, and even a few airport coffee locations. By the grace of God, my business enterprise survived the 2008 financial crisis and the 2020 COVID-19 global pandemic. Just like the story of Job in the Bible, God blessed me with more than I'd lost. I am grateful for my journey, all of it.

What's the takeaway here? Don't be afraid of change. Whether it be a choice or a change forced upon you, accept it, reflect on it, go to a peaceful place to clear your mind, and identify and plan your next New Thing.

For me, prayer is the guide that opens my mind and provides clarity during times of uncertainty.

This is my mantra of inspiration. I am gifting it to you to write in your journal and reflect on throughout your life:

Find your seat at the table; if there isn't one, pull one up, or better yet, build your own table.

It is all about building for me.

Don't worry; I'm not telling you to quit your job and open your own business today. Whether you are a blue-collar worker, a white-collar worker, an entrepreneur, or even a creative, I encourage you to step out of your comfort zone once a month to build strength and confidence; taste, experience, feel, take a deep breath, and put yourself out there. When you open yourself up to New Things, you make space for Divine Order to bring things you couldn't even imagine were possible into your life.

You may be quite happy being content, but being content will not push you to grow. You may be totally buried in a routine that has you stuck, not realizing that if you just start something new, you will open yourself up to receiving greater opportunities or epiphanies. It may seem like a risk, but these changes are needed for the growth you seek, the balance you crave, and the new vibe and outlook that will get you that promotion you have been chasing.

Starting with little changes, you can move yourself into a more comfortable frame of mind, going somewhere else where you can be seen and allowing yourself to thrive. New Things will open up new pathways. Now, you've put yourself in a place to be noticed by the boss who's previously overlooked you or to pursue the dream you've been deferring. They'll see you for who you really are, or it'll open up another opportunity, because you're now open to receiving other prospects, bringing you the confidence to take it and say yes.

Once you commit to embracing change in your career, your business, and yourself, your newfound openness will cause others to see you differently as well. The world will see you and nurture you, too. You'll be more comfortable making the changes you need to make. With each incremental change, you will move past fear toward the best, most fulfilled version of yourself.

EXERCISES:

The main topics of this chapter are accepting change and feeding your soul.

1. Review your current work situation. How are you feeling about it? Are there new areas you wish you could explore or goals you want to reach? What new skills, experience, or continuing education would you need to enhance your work situation?

2. Make a list of factors that may be holding you back from your professional goals. Pick one and write the steps you must take to overcome it. Once you've made moves to reach your goals, update your resume to see how you have changed.

3. What type of training would make you more desirable for a promotion or new job? New skills or certifications? Interpersonal or social skills?

4. What can you do to feed and renew your soul? Some ideas include taking a personal day to do something fun like going out into nature, reading books, listening to podcasts, or seeking a creative outlet to enrich your soul. Whatever route you choose, take some time to reflect.

3

FINDING YOUR HAPPY PLACE

What is it in your life that brings you peace and joy? For some, it could be a hobby, a passion project, or a special place. Your happy place might not be one thing. It could be several different things. For instance, the place where you do your hobby could be your happy place, where you do your happy thing. Your she-shed or man-cave may be that place, and the thing you do there is the happy activity. Reading, sewing, writing, painting figurines for Warhammer or a model train set, quilting, or whatever activity makes you happy.

A sure way to grow the positivity in your life is to double down on the places and activities you know you enjoy. If you already enjoy something, maybe your New Thing could be to do that happy activity in a whole new way or take it to the next level. For example, one friend loves gardening so she can have fresh herbs and vegetables for cooking. However, with her work schedule, she is not able to tend to a garden daily, and her herbs would die off during winter or not be as robust. For her New Thing, she set up a system with a grow light in her home office. Now, she has fresh herbs and vegetables year-round, bringing nature's tranquility to her workspace. So, while she can't always have the enjoyment of working in a garden, her garden has moved in with her year-round, and her plants thrive because she begins her day by tending to their care.

Why is this important? Just as it is important to feed your body and soul, you must also tend to your mental wellness. Setting yourself in the right mindset will put you on the path to accomplishing many New Things. Your old thing you did when you were young, which you may not have time for in your adult life, may be done in a new way as an adult. Creating your happy place to do what you love gives you a way to escape, reenergize, and reflect.

Your happy place may be your own backyard, patio, or even balcony you can convert into a relaxing refuge. If you don't have a place to go where you live, this may be the time to begin the project that has been percolating in the back of your mind. Your New Thing could be to create or carve out that new place for your happy activity, even if it's just creating a reading corner or finding a nearby park you can visit regularly.

Some people like to do their happy activity with their partner, a friend, or a group of people who share their same passion. This interaction is healthy and builds social skills and community. This activity could be through a club, church, synagogue, or other entity. Just by regularly participating you will stimulate your mental acuity and bond with others. The activity could be anything from playing chess to participating in a sports league. (We will explore group activities in Chapter Six.)

In other cases, a person's happy place or activity could be something solitary, away from the hustle and bustle of the world. The place might be in the privacy of their home or in nature, and the activity could be something quiet and individual. Many people need this time to unwind from their daily grind, recharge, and rejuvenate their soul, and that need is just as important as social connection.

For me, any place with water, like the ocean, beach, lake, or a waterfall, is my happy place. For me, touching the ocean is like touching God's hand. Wherever I go and find a body of water, I must dip my hands or feet in and swim. And swimming outside is definitely a happy place for me. So, places like Fiji, Ghana, Greece, or the Italian Riviera—places near water—feed my soul. I used to think that Greece and the Italian Riviera were my favorite places in the world until I went to Fiji. I found the people there are the nicest and happiest people on the planet. You can't even start the day in Fiji unless you say, "*bula, bula*," meaning "good day," to everyone you see. Fijians are the kindest people living in the most beautiful land.

Because I'm not able to visit Fiji every day, I decided to create a Fiji-inspired relaxing retreat in my backyard. The idea lived on my vision board for ten years until I decided to tackle it as one of my New Things. Now, in the private oasis in my backyard, I can find peace and relax close to home on my own terms. My own sanctuary. My happy place.

Then there are my happy places inside my home, areas where I can steal away to write. Notice the plural: My writing place is not always one set spot—where I settle depends on my mood in the moment. I move around to different comfy places in my home, jumping from couch to corner to kitchen table. But never in the bedroom, because my professional and life coaches say that the bedroom is for rest, not work.

One place I really didn't expect to be a happy place for me is Las Vegas. It's a city where I have received the best news and had good things happen to me, but also where I had to start over, struggle, and dig deep. While living in Vegas, I deepened my spiritual connection to God. I was rebaptized as an adult in Vegas, and it is the place where my son was created. Now, when I think about Vegas, I remember it as the place where I clearly heard God speak to me for the first time. Surprisingly enough, even with all the losses I experienced in Las Vegas, ironically, it is still one of my happy places.

Another way to make way for your happy place is to purge the clutter that stops you from enjoying life. Life is so full of things that collect dust, piles that we ignore, junk drawers we don't want to open, and mailers. (Oh, my goodness, so many mailers!) When we are able to remove the clutter, we can feel free and spacious enough to accept new thoughts and ideas and let our creativity grow.

For some people, a vision board can help build a visualization of the New Thing you would like to do, a place you would like to create, or even somewhere you've always dreamed of visiting. You can start a vision board with something you may already have, such as a corkboard, whiteboard, or scrapbook, or even create one on your phone with apps like Pinterest. Visualizing your New Thing, or writing about it in your journal, is the first step to making your New Thing a reality.

Each person's journey to a happy place or activity is unique and essential. Some mental health professionals suggest meditation, yoga, or a mindful walk, but what works for one may not work for another. Finding the method that resonates with you is crucial and can lead you to a healthier way of relaxing and rejuvenating. Therefore, it's important to keep exploring until you find the place, activity, or thing that allows you to open your mind to the visualization of your dreams.

My mom, who is a medical professional and Psychiatric Registered Nurse (RN) specializing in mental health, has been involved with my 12 New Things Lifestyle adventures since the start. With her professional background and her own 12 New Things journey, I thought her perspective would be a good addition, especially in this chapter. These are my mother's reflections, shared in her own words:

As Shonda's mom, I have had the pleasure of experiencing the birth of the 12 New Things. 12 New Things as a lifestyle can help you recognize the daily joys of life. You begin to see how many New Things you experience each day. As a walker, daily I see the magnificence of God on my nature walks. I usually walk near bodies of water to maintain my peace of mind. It is important to connect with nature as a way to maintain mental wellness. On my walks, I look across the bay, lake, creek, or ocean to connect with God and realize how much God loves me. I am created just as these bodies of water by the Supreme Being, God. With each day, I am regenerated to see, feel, think, hear, taste the wonders of life. 12 New Things helps me reflect on this wonderful gift of life I have.

There's a saying, "When negativity tries to enter your person, think of the positive opposite." The more I practice this the better I feel. Even the folks around you start recognizing the benefits of your positive energy.

12 New Things has been a road map for me, the guide to help you achieve these things. The 12 New Things Lifestyle renews my heart and mind to appreciate the wonders of my life! I appreciate the wonders I've experienced so far and those I've yet to explore! I am grateful for the 12 New Things challenge.

Mommy in the early days working as a registered nurse

Being a Psychiatric nurse can be stressful, and 12 New Things has been very beneficial to me. I walk and during my walks I have found myself looking for New Things right in my environment. It's amazing how many small but wonderful things I find: new flowers; ravens flying over my backyard; the deer who would come to the area behind my home, lie down and rest, or munch on my flowers looking at me as if I'm a stranger. Additionally, my daughter, Shonda, has expanded my experiences by inviting me to share some of her New Things with exploring new countries. Each New Thing has expanded my physical, emotional, and spiritual being. It has made me more youthful, more excited as I age.

Finding your happy place is an important step toward engaging and illuminating the path to your inner peace and wellness. Having this place away from the distractions of life will bring you solace, clearing your mind to make way for new thoughts, creativity, and growth in your life. For me, I know my happy place continues to be a source for renewal.

EXERCISES:

1. To free your mind for your New Thing, identify a space in your home that has clutter. Take time to purge and organize.

2. Make a list of your hobbies and things that have made you happy over your lifetime. How could you approach these activities in a new way to deepen your enjoyment of them as time goes on?

3. Make a list of the places that make you happy and why. If any are places that you can't visit regularly, how might you bring their best elements closer to home?

4. Make your vision board. This can be used to create a new space in your home or yard or even to plan a trip. Look for images from magazines, brochures, websites, social media, or other sources that fit your vision of what you want your happy place and New Thing to be. Pin them to a corkboard, paste them in a scrapbook, or save them to a digital board or desktop—some place you'll see it regularly. Keep building your vision, and you'll be surprised at how quickly the Universe sets things in motion!

"Thy word is a lamp to my feet and a light to my path."
—Psalms 119:105

4

THAT'S WHAT FRIENDS ARE FOR

What are friends for? Having friends at a young age was essential for the development of our social skills. When we are young, playing with friends helps us learn how to work out issues, care, share, and trust. Throughout childhood, we're constantly trying New Things with friends because everything is new. Then, as adults, we tend to step back and rarely try anything new because it's easier to stick with what we know, and we're too busy, too tired, or too stressed. So, how can you use the 12 New Things Lifestyle to make and keep friendships strong as an adult? And what is a true friend anyway?

A true, good friend, not just an acquaintance, is someone you can genuinely rely on to love you and support you uncon-ditionally. Someone who, no matter the distance between you, when you reconnect, it always feels like no time has passed. What does it really take to nurture and maintain a long-term friendship? How can you tell which friends are in your life to stay for the long haul? And how can we know when and how to let go of the ones that aren't really good for us? The 12 New Things Lifestyle can help you to strengthen a good relationship, breathe new life into a faded friendship, or do New Things to form new friendships that open your life up to new possibilities.

Every friendship has its rough patches, even the oldest and closest ones that go back to our childhood, school days, or first job. Maintaining friendships is not easy because friends and circumstances evolve over time, especially once we leave home, start work, and grow up into our true selves. As we become young adults, we begin to spend most of our waking hours at work. Work demands such as long hours, frequent travel, or relocation to a new city, plus whatever mode of home life we're in at that time (single, dating, married, with or without kids), start to shape our days. As a result, some good friends may be lost along the way.

I have a few good friends I grew up with through high school. Somehow, we lost touch, not because of some falling out, but simply because we went different ways through college and career. Then, years later, we suddenly found ourselves living in the same community. Some were married, and many of us had kids who all landed at the same high school, which brought us all back together again. We had the chance to renew our old friendships, and bringing our families together made those relationships evolve into whole new dynamics filled with fond memories of when we were our children's age.

These friendships sprung up again by lucky happenstance, but you can use the 12 New Things concept to intentionally rekindle lost friendships too. One of my girlfriends has a friend she grew up with, and the two of them have shared a love of the same boy band since they were kids. Even though they live in different parts of the country, they meet wherever the band is back together again. They make it a fun weekend of activities in whatever place in the world the band happens to be performing.

During Beyoncé's Renaissance Tour, thousands of fans, including me, used this New Thing to connect with loved ones at "away from home" tour stops to enjoy the show together. Our shared love of the music gave us a reason to get together and served as a catalyst for those distant friendships.

And this doesn't just apply to friends in distant locations. Exploring New Things is a great way to deepen any friendship by giving you new experiences to connect over. You and a friend can make a plan to do something together you both have never done before or tackle a New Thing in a more significant way, like being each other's gym accountability buddies. Or your friend may have something they enjoy doing all of the time, but you haven't joined them in that activity before. They may rave about the Dungeons & Dragons campaigns they're playing or a place they love to travel to, but you've only experienced it through their stories. Their thing could be your New Thing, which could bring you closer and create new memories.

One of my friends bought a home in Martha's Vineyard, a place I had always wanted to go but had never been to before. After years of knowing this friend, I booked a trip to Martha's Vineyard during a time when my friend was on the island. She hosted me on my stay, and we created a new memory after decades of friendship. These bonding experiences are precious moments in time, securing your relationship for those occasions when one of you may need someone to rely on.

As life comes at you head on, it's inevitable in every friendship that one of you will need to be strong in the moment, helping the other with all sorts of things. Good friends are those who are gladly there for you, but part of being a good friend is also recognizing when a friend needs you to be their pillar. Is this something you're already doing in your friendships, or could it be your New Thing? Say a friend suddenly starts acting odd, becoming somewhat elusive, not communicating, and maybe even dropping out of sight for a while. This could be a sign they are moving away from the friendship, or they're struggling with an issue they do not want to reveal. They might be suffering from a personal tragedy, dealing with an illness, or have some situation they don't want to burden a friend with. If this is a friend you want to nurture your relationship with, you could take on the task of supporting them as your New Thing. With a bit of careful investigation or gentle inquiry, you could try to find out what's going on with them. This friend may need your support through a trying time, especially if they have been there for you. This New Thing project could strengthen your bond and open you both up to a deeper level of friendship.

Sometimes, you may have a friendship somewhere in your life that has suffered a terrible circumstance that sent both of you to different corners. I have two friends who were inseparable from grade school through high school, and they still kept in touch through college and beyond. Then, one day, at an event at one of their homes, they simply had it out. There must have been some underlying issue that just tore the friendship apart. Everyone who attended the event to this day just cannot understand what happened. While we wonder and have tried to help set up a mediation, they both prefer to not see or hear from each other. To begin with, this friendship could have been toxic, one-sided, or competitive, and they may never have been true friends to begin with. Maybe one day after more time passes, they may find each other again.

On the other hand, it just may be better to sever a toxic friendship before it gets to the point of a heated battle. Some personalities just may not mesh with one another—like oil and water. The always-negative person, the person who always has to be right, or the one who's always the showoff may not be able to enjoy the other friend's good times. In reviewing your friends, what New Thing can you do to let go of a toxic or negative person in your life?

More importantly, you can use the 12 New Things to breathe fresh life into true friendships to strengthen your most cherished relationships for the future. For a friend who has been your strong supporter through thick and thin, you could do something special with them. Plan a spa day, take them out to lunch, visit a museum, enjoy afternoon high tea, or go shopping. Think about doing something fun with that friend where the two of you can be together forming new and cherished memories.

A bigger New Thing could be planning a trip with several friends and having them invite their friends, bringing together people who may not know each other so everyone can meet new friends as well. You all could do a cruise, go to a resort, travel to attend an event, or whatever brings all of you together with new experiences and activities for the group.

I've had friends who I have lost contact with. Then we find ourselves back together because of a life tragedy or a milestone event like a wedding. One particular friend and I started having meetups once a quarter. Our quarterly dates are when we do all our catching up with each other over lunch or dinner. We laugh about old times and catch up on the things happening in our lives. These intentional meet-ups are so important for keeping our friendship even as life circumstances keep us apart, and that's really the key: being intentional about it.

I attended a live interview between Oprah and forever First Lady Michelle Obama where they discussed Oprah's planning of Mrs. Obama's fiftieth birthday party. Oprah asked the First Lady to bring her closest friends, and Mrs. Obama said, "Okay." When Oprah followed up with, "How many people?" Mrs. Obama replied, "Well, it's like twelve." Oprah was skeptical. "You don't have twelve good friends," she said. Mrs. Obama confirmed, "Yes, I do, I do." Oprah countered, "Who has twelve good friends? I got Gayle." But then Oprah met Michelle's "kitchen table," as she affectionately refers to her close circle of friends, and she immediately saw how the former First Lady collects and keeps special friends throughout life. They are an assortment of people who keep her grounded. Over the years, Mrs. Obama has worked on these relationships, not as a convenience, but more as an intentional commitment.[1]

If you and your friends have trust, compassion, honesty, and independence, you already have the foundation of a

---

1   Michelle Obama and Oprah Winfrey, "'Barack Is My Home' with Oprah Winfrey," April 25, 2023, in *Michelle Obama: The Light Podcast*, podcast.

strong and healthy friendship. Even though it can be hard to recognize when a friendship is weak in some areas, it is always possible to improve yourself and your relationship with a friend. Is your friend there for you and you for them? Do you really listen to each other? It takes time to nurture and develop these qualities. Some people make friends quickly, and others may be more hesitant, perhaps having been hurt by a friend in the past, but growing and maintaining any friendship takes effort and commitment.

We also have different relationships at different times in our lives. For instance, what it takes to be a good friend in grade school is much different from what makes a good friend in high school. A group of preschoolers may view a new friend as someone to go on mystical adventures with. One day they are playing with animals, and the next, they are fighting dinosaurs together. Friendships in middle school and high school become more complex as you begin to need someone to confide in about crushes and other coming-of-age situations. As we mature, so do our relationships with our friends. The best friendships last through all kinds of life-changing situations, evolving as time goes by.

Do you know what kind of friends you have, what kind of friend you are, and what you should do to strengthen each friendship? Are you the friend who is there helping them move to a new place, celebrating a new relationship, or supporting them in times of loss? Understanding your friends' lives and family dynamics and being truly happy for and enjoying your friends' accomplishments is being a good friend. What New Thing can you do to strengthen your friendships? We all can do something better to build and bolster the friendships we have in our lives.

Which friendships are the longest?

Which friendships are the strongest?

Which friends were you once close to but have lost touch with?

It may have been because one of you moved away, went to college, or simply dove into their career or family and didn't keep in contact. Find that person to see where they are today in their life, where they are located now, and see if you both are wanting to reconnect. Staying in contact is so much easier today with texting, email, and social media. Back in our parents' and grandparents' days, they had to actually write letters on paper that they then had to send by mail or make long-distance phone calls, which were expensive, and hope the other person was at home to answer. So, in this day and age, we have no excuse to not keep in touch.

It will take time, patience, and open communication, but it will be a blessing to build and bond with your core true friend group and to plan adventures with individual friends as well. It's time to break out of your everyday routine and try a New Thing with a friend—and who knows what new friends you might make along the way?

EXERCISES:

1. Make a list of those people you consider friends today. Out of that list, who is in your core group? Is there one friend who is your best and closest? Are there friends you wish you were closer to?

2. Make a list of new activities you could do with your core group. It could be something casual, like a themed potluck where each dinner guest makes and brings one component of the meal (appetizers, mains, sides, drinks, dessert, etc.), a day hike, or an activity class like sushi making, yoga, or baking. Or it could be something bigger like a vacation cruise, a weekend getaway, or a recurring commitment like a running group. Whatever the New Thing is, the point is to have an activity where everyone is able to enjoy each other's company in a new, fun way.

3. Make a list of activities you can do one-on-one with a close friend or a friend you're trying to get closer to. Think about asking them to be your walking buddy, go for a spa day, visit a museum, or volunteer together.

4. Plan to invite one friend to join you for an event to enjoy together. Decide on an activity and date and reach out to that friend to get the ball rolling.

5. When you have found that one friend you enjoy doing New Things with, plan to make it a recurring thing, whether that's monthly or whatever fits into each of your lives.

"One who has unreliable friends soon comes to ruin,
but there is a friend who sticks closer than a brother."

—Proverbs 18:24

5

GUESS WHO'S (ALL) COMING TO DINNER

One cannot think well, love well,
sleep well, if one has not dined well.

—Virginia Woolf

If you think about it, almost every major life event has a food element to it: marriage, birthdays, holidays, and even death. Food is healing: It's a way of sharing cultures, and, of course, it's life-sustaining. There are also the restorative powers and the comforting effect of food like chicken noodle soup. It's how we show love, how we celebrate, and how we connect—with family members and strangers alike.

When I was growing up, my parents always had big gatherings with lots of food at our home. There was always some extended family staying at our house, and more would come for holidays. Food was not only the focal point of the family but also the core of the family business. I have many fond childhood memories of the smell of fresh homemade rolls, of baking peach cobbler, and of making crispy fried chicken on Sundays. These are all recipes that have been passed down in my family for generations.

Sitting down for a meal is also the way we all communicate about everything from the happenings from the day—what went on at work and school—to sharing family stories. So, it's no wonder that when I began to have my own parties, they would all have a theme and lots of food. So many memories of barbeques, pool parties, and taco bars. As I grew older and became a mom, as I immersed myself in raising my son and growing my business, the parties became fewer, and I became a bit more guarded about opening my home for huge gatherings.

And more recently, it's not just that we've all gotten busy and lost touch. Due to COVID-19, many people, especially the young ones, have lost out on the social interaction and connection that large gatherings for meals and parties bring—and with it, the chance to build skills around meeting new people. Due to this isolation, many people now suffer from social anxiety. The conveniences of buying everything from groceries to pharmacy items without needing to come in contact with another human have erected new walls and barriers to meeting new people, public speaking, being around strangers, and even everyday situations like speaking to the cashier at the local market. Many people had jobs that were changed from in-office to remote, which removed the opportunities for social interactions—chatting around the water cooler or eating together in the lunchroom.

One way to overcome these anxieties around new people would be to expose yourself to situations out of your comfort zone. Find a way to get together with people you don't know. The more strangers you open yourself up to, the more you will be able to open yourself up to new ideas. This brings us to exploring your next New Thing and how breaking bread with others can also break down the particular barriers that protect but separate you.

For instance, when President and Mrs. Obama launched the Obama Foundation in Chicago after finishing their second term in the White House, they kicked it off with a two-day summit. Their plan was for the foundation to become the hub of the Obama Presidential Center, which would include a museum, conference center, and educational project. It was to be a place where they could build their legacy and honor the stories of the people who supported their journey. I was invited to attend the summit, along with hundreds of people from various backgrounds from all over the world. We attended seminars, panel sessions, and workshops, followed by a communal dinner.

For the dinner portion of the evening, the organization randomly assigned strangers to sit together in groups of twelve. The rule was you were not seated with anyone you knew. Folks who came to the summit together were all separated and assigned to different tables. Each table was a mix of all ages, colors, and lifestyles, filling the vast room with tables of twelve strangers.

The table I was assigned to was composed of people from all over the United States. We ranged in age from thirty to sixty and formed a clever mix of races with differing backgrounds. There was a lawyer from New York, a restaurateur from Miami, and my favorite, the executive director of the African American Museum. She was most interesting, and I was amazed at her extensive knowledge of the rich African American history the museum's holdings represented. We were all immediately put at ease and engaged in meaningful conversations, thanks in part to the question cards provided at each table. The point of the dinner was to demonstrate that we had more commonalities than differences.

The whole weekend was an amazing experience, and I came away with such a sense of wanting to bring these concepts into my own life. I immediately thought that the dinner part of the event could be a perfect project for one of my 12 New Things adventures. Wanting to organize my own community dinner with twelve strangers was a feeling that stayed with me and I couldn't shake off. I was inspired, and now I just had to figure out how to pull it off.

As I began to think about what I would do, the excitement and fun ideas started to battle with certain apprehensions. I'm really a very private person, so I didn't necessarily know how I would host this type of communal dinner at my home with strangers coming into my living space. That was a big question. Then, social anxiety began to creep in about how I could make this work. And safety. I mean, who was I going to invite, and how would I find these people? You can't just walk up to someone on the street and say, "Hey! How would you like to come to my house for dinner?" How was I going to find the connecting factor that would make this doable?

With other things going on at the time, I decided to file the idea away to figure out later. I really didn't want to forget such a fun event that was such a good idea for one of my 12 New Things activities. And it was still in my heart to do it, so I prayed on it, believing something would eventually be revealed to me.

Then, months later, I'm checking my email, and I notice a message from the UCLA Alumni Association with the subject line: "Dinner with 12 Strangers." I thought, *Oh, my goodness, there it is, a way for me to do the 12 New Things dinner with strangers!* The beauty of UCLA Alumni's Dinner with 12 Strangers is that it is hosted by alumni, and you can sign up to be a host or a participant. The email read, "Dinner with 12 Strangers is an over fifty-year UCLA tradition that has become a global phenomenon. Every year, over three nights, alums, faculty, and students come together to enjoy good food and great conversation." The email mentioned that over the past year, alums hosted more than 500 dinners around the world, involving more than 3,700 Bruins. It went on to say that dinners could be hosted for students near UCLA or for fellow alumni here in Oakland, around the country, and around the world! Brilliant!

The funny thing is I had been receiving these emails for years and never noticed any of them until now, when I was open to the 12 New Things Lifestyle. So, you never know. One of your 12 New Things adventures could be waiting for you right in your inbox.

This was perfect! As a host, you have no idea who will sign up to attend your dinner. The attendees select the event they want to go to in their area. This was the perfect combination, to do both a 12 New Things activity and reconnect with other UCLA alumni, and I felt it was a safer way to accomplish this community dinner with strangers. I immediately signed up to be a host.

I started to get into party mode and began planning. Although a potluck is a wonderful and appropriate way to host Dinner with 12 Strangers, I wanted to do something different. I immediately thought this would be a great way to highlight my friend Chef Michele McQueen's business. She is a caterer, and she would not only help me create the perfect menu, but she was also someone I grew up with and trusted. She is now a celebrity chef who owns her own restaurant. I have hired her to cater many events, so I knew she could come up with a great way to execute my idea.

I thought, *You are together for two hours with strangers. What do you do?*

My plan was to have everyone pair up to cook various dishes at different stations. I had done something similar at an event at a cooking school, and it was a great experience. Cooking together would be a perfect way for us to bond.

After the event was posted, I was excited to see the people signing up. I didn't know who they were, just that they weren't people I personally knew. One person asked if their wife could attend because she was also an alum, and I said, "Of course!" They had met at UCLA and gotten married years ago. I also heard from people who knew me and saw I was hosting the dinner. They wanted to join the fun, but I had to explain that no, it was all about getting twelve strangers together, and I encouraged them to find another dinner at the home of someone they did not know to stay true to the tradition. I was thrilled when my event booked up.

Chef Michele and I worked together, planning and developing the menu. I rented all the dining items, such as plates, stemware, and utensils. We were trying to think of everything to make the evening go smoothly without having a ton of cleaning to deal with at the end. At first, I planned to have the dinner outside in a tent, but the weather soon kiboshed that idea. Then, as I looked around my house, I began to notice things that needed attention. I completed a tile project I had been wanting to do for years, got some walls painted, and moved furniture around to fit a long table that could seat everyone comfortably. I also changed around the art and found places for new pieces that I hadn't put up yet. (Just one more example of how doing one New Thing can kickstart other projects!)

The day finally arrived. Everything was well thought out, down to the aprons. I had the front entrance decorated with UCLA Bruin blue- and yellow-colored lights so everyone could find the house easily and to ensure school spirit started upon arrival. The table was carefully set with the dishes and stemware and decorated with floral arrangements and candles. Anticipation grew, as I didn't really know the people who were coming. Although I had their names and emails to provide event details, I did not know how any of the guests' personalities would be, how the conversation would flow, or how the group would get along. In hindsight, there wasn't anything to worry about.

As the guests arrived, they were greeted with UCLA Bruin blue Champagne and cucumber mint-infused water. Everyone signed in and put on a special name tag with the logo for the

UCLA Dinner with 12 Strangers event. The couple arrived. Then, coincidentally, two other guests who were doctors who knew each other but didn't know they had both attended UCLA or were even attending the dinner that night arrived.

Most of the guests were originally from the Los Angeles area. One had just moved to the Bay Area, and another, who was a writer for a reputable newspaper, was in Oakland to cover a play for a story she was working on. One was a neighbor who lived literally half a mile from my house. We had never met before, and she didn't realize the dinner would be so close to her home. She had a stable at her home and jokingly said she could have ridden one of her horses to the dinner. She kindly invited me to go horseback riding with her through our neighborhood as one of my 12 New Things adventures. I still have to take her up on the offer, but this is another example of how opening the door to one new adventure can lead to other ones you never dreamed of.

Once everyone arrived, we played an icebreaker game. Everyone picked five M&M's, then we all went around and each selected one color out of the five. Each color had an icebreaker question associated with it. For instance, brown was "Tell us something about yourself that most people do not know about you." It was a perfect way to learn about each other and helped everyone bond immediately. Then it was time to get cooking. We pulled names to team up for the cooking stations. Chef Michele had prepared recipes and the ingredients for each station. I worked on the shrimp and blue grits with the young woman who had recently graduated and moved to the Bay Area. Chef gave us the history of blue grits and showed us how to make stock with the shrimp shells. The other teams worked on macaroni and cheese, greens, and Southern fried chicken.

Chef came around to each station to observe our techniques and coach us. She also gave us cooking tips like chewing gum while chopping onions so you don't tear up. (Who knew?) Since she had become a part of our crew, we invited her to eat with us as an honorary Bruin, although she was a Bison—an alumna of Howard University, a historically Black university. That night we were all one big happy family: cooking, dining, and laughing together.

At dinner, we had question cards similar to those from the Obama dinner to help us reminisce about our UCLA experiences. We talked about where we lived during our undergraduate studies. We talked about parts of campus where we had classes. One of the guests had worked in my favorite campus coffeehouse in Ackerman Union, and I learned how they made my favorite coffee drink, Cafe Royale. I enjoyed it so much that I had it as a special drink on the menu at my coffeehouse in Las Vegas. Turns out the secret ingredient is Mexican chocolate. We all relived our time at UCLA, going over fond memories and making new ones. Several of the guests discussed a famous Mexican place in

Hayward, California. We thought it would be fun to get back together and made a commitment to meet there for Cinco de Mayo.

What was so wonderful about our experience was cooking together and eating family-style, which brought an instant bond. We all let our hair down to enjoy the experience and have a great time. I enjoyed hosting the dinner. The joy of people laughing and having a good time makes me happy. At the end of the night, we closed with the famous UCLA eight-clap, and I ended with a toast: "We came as strangers and left as friends." Cheers!

Now, how would you go about finding a way to have dinner with strangers in your own home? Well, if you aren't a UCLA alum, then think about the organizations you are involved with or the hobbies you enjoy. In my research for this, I ran across multiple websites that help people host community dinners for people with similar interests. Or, if you'd rather not host, there are groups that advertise communal dinners you can attend. So, with a bit of careful research, you may find an organization that can open you up to all sorts of new connections.

If you are not ready to host a dinner or to stroll into someone else's home, solo travel is a great way to connect with strangers on a smaller level. Dining alone in hotels opens up doors to meeting new people. When I find myself out eating alone, I sometimes strike up conversations with people in the waiting area or at a nearby table. In a lot of restaurants, single diners often sit at the bar, so you'll be in good company with friendly neighbors nearby.

One time during a trip to Los Angeles, I found this amazing luxury café with an eight-course dinner complete with wine pairings. I decided to book a table and enjoy the experience alone as my New Thing for that month. It just so happened there was a handsome young man, about my son's age, sitting alone a couple of tables away. He noticed I was also alone and came over.

He explained that he was supposed to have this experience with his mom for a Mother's Day gift, but she had to go on a business trip abroad, so he was by himself.

He asked, "Do you mind if we dine together?"

He was enjoying the same eight-course dinner, and we happened to be on the same course. I thought, *Hey, this is perfect for one of my 12 New Things,* so I told him, "Sure!" I added, "You must be an old soul because this is something that people did back in the day." I wondered if he was drawn to me because I'm a businesswoman like his mom.

It was funny when the waiters noticed the young man had shifted over to my table. One waiter approached with his plate of food and a surprised look. Carefully positioning himself behind my new dining companion in such a way so he could mouth only to me, "Is this okay with you?" I assured the waiter that I was fine with it.

It was quite an event. The courses began with sparkling wine paired with an appetizer with foam and caviar, then julienned veggies with a warm broth, wagyu beef that had aged for nine hours wrapped in filo, and dessert with a honeycomb and cream called "milk and honey." Everything was artfully designed and plated, and the wine pairings were perfect.

Later the young man became my new friend on Instagram and committed to the 12 New Things Lifestyle. The 12 New Things has opened me up to so many new experiences and new people with interesting stories.

EXERCISES:

1. Make a list of different ways you might meet new people. For instance, through your alumni network; through a club, church, or synagogue you belong to; or through your friends.

2. Research different events in your area where you can connect with people over food. For starters, you might look into cooking classes, wine tastings, or similar events.

3. Plan a lunch or dinner event at your home and invite twelve people from different times in your life. Try to select people who don't necessarily know each other

to have a diverse group. Assign each participant a different part of a large salad that they will prepare at your event. And don't forget the icebreaker questions to spur conversation.

4. If you would like to go bigger, try hosting a dinner like I did through an organization you are connected with or something close to your heart you are involved in. (You may need to do some research to find an organization you care about and trust.) Remember to take notes in your journal throughout your planning and recap your experience afterward with your takeaway thoughts and memories. After you have completed this New Thing, share with us on social media and save the memories for future reflection.

"Behold, I stand at the door and knock. If anyone hears my voice and opens the door, I will come in to him and eat with him, and he with me."
—Revelation 3:20

6

LEVELING UP LIKE
STEPH CURRY

Taking care of oneself mentally and physically is a key component of the 12 New Things Lifestyle, especially for those who've historically neglected themselves to care for others. Remember what I wrote earlier about those unfulfilled New Year's resolutions? Dieting, exercise, and self-care are always right up there with quitting smoking and drinking less when it comes to hollow commitments that people try on briefly and then drop in short order. One main reason for this attrition rate is that people tend to set goals that are far too ambitious. Time and again, it's been proven that developing small, good habits over the short term is the best way to successfully make bigger changes and better ourselves in the long run. We need to build a self-care practice into our lives that will sustain us for years to come. Caring for others must begin with self-care to endure and be effective—as the saying goes, you can't pour out of an empty cup.

Stubbornness and old habits often get in the way of our finding the best routines, therapies, and treatments. We're also all very different in terms of what works for our bodies. One type of exercise or diet may work for one person but not another. Everyone's genetics and body chemistry are different. Just because your friend happens to drop weight from a new diet or exercise regimen, don't be too quick to hop on board the same train. Be thoughtful about it and find your own New Thing. And you don't have to completely change your whole lifestyle to do it. In fact, it would be better if you did just one little New Thing for a month and make it your regular thing if it works. If not, you can try another New Thing the next month. Then you are not throwing off your whole lifestyle for some unknown, crazy life-changing diet or exercise plan that you will soon grow tired of and then quit. Take it slow and add on as you go. This way, the little victories will mean so much more, and you might find the New Thing will become your life thing that you can't live without.

In order to be prepared to take on any of our 12 New Things challenges, we must take care of our physical bodies. During the COVID-19 lockdown, in an attempt to stay active, I tried a dance fitness class called Samba Funk, which I could do in my backyard over Zoom. It's like a combination of samba dance using soul and rock music in an African-inspired fitness experience. You move your feet, arms, and hips in a fast motion to the music. In my research, I found that samba was actually against the law around a hundred years ago. It was thought to be the music of former slaves, and you could be arrested for even playing it. So crazy! And so fascinating . . .

There are also ancient Eastern forms of proven therapy, such as yoga and tai chi. I have taken yoga since 1995 and recently tried virtual yoga for the first time. Virtual classes are a great way to stay in shape if you are not able to get out to a gym, if there are no class offerings in your area, or if you simply prefer to work out at home. Numerous virtual options are available to you to help keep your body in shape in fun new ways. If you are a senior needing a lower intensity workout, there are classes available through SilverSneakers and other programs that offer all levels of programs to fit your needs and capabilities. Again, it's better to do something than nothing. For my regular exercise, I swim, ride my Peloton bike, or walk with my "granddog," Rico, at least thirty to forty minutes each day. When I am traveling, I stay at hotels with pools so I can swim even while I'm on the road. Recently, I have incorporated Pilates into my exercise routine, and I love it. I have never been into stretching; Pilates is exactly what I need.

What do you love about your current routine, and what would you like to add? Your New Thing could be to try an activity like pickleball or some other sport that gets you moving physically and engaging socially. No matter what age you are, these activities with others hit the mark for so many things you need to keep your body healthy while feeding your mind and soul. This healthy New Thing, done with friends, is a way to get in touch with your much-needed physical needs and build healthy friendships. Also, doing an activity with friends is more likely to become a regular thing because you're there to encourage each other to stay consistent. Whereas if you're exercising alone at home, you're more likely to stray away or skip the workout for the day.

I used to weigh myself all the time at home, then divinely, my scale broke, and I stopped. Now I rarely weigh myself and focus more on being healthy. As a former model, I spent half my life worried about my weight, to the point of developing an eating disorder when I was in high school. I hid my struggle from my family for years. It took me diving deeper into my faith and realizing that the road to perfection is not what God intended for us. God knows we are imperfect and loves us through our imperfections. This powerful revelation was life-changing and lifesaving for me. Growing deeper in my faith led me to become more focused on how to like myself and be the best me I could be. Nowadays, 12 New Things is the platform I use to encourage everyone to embrace change in fun, positive ways—to be your best self in health, career, family, and every other area of your life.

For one of my New Things, I wanted to eat healthier, so I decided to try going vegan. There are so many healthy options now for plant-based foods. I found that the grocery stores by me have vegan options in almost every category. The freezer section has everything from plant-based burgers to vegan bacon. I even saw buffalo wing "veggitizers" and pizza made with vegan cheese. It's incredible, the breadth of choices, many of them so good you can barely tell the difference. One of your 12 New Things in this area could be to make taste comparisons between the real thing and whatever healthier version you want to try, whether that's plant-based, gluten free, lower sodium, or whatever, and then begin replacing a meal or two throughout the week with that healthy option.

Right before the pandemic, I began following an Atlanta eatery called Slutty Vegan on Instagram. They have a menu of a variety of vegan burgers and a line that stretches out the door and down the street. So, when I was in Atlanta, I planned for extra time to stand in line to try the Slutty Vegan burger as my New Thing for that month. The menu was so creative, with fun options and crazy names. I tried one of their burgers called the "Fussy Hussy." It was so good that I didn't even think to ask, "Where's the beef?"

Trying Slutty Vegan made me want to find more creative ways to adopt a plant-based diet. And, to top it off, I'm inspired by the thirtysomething African American owner and founder of Slutty Vegan, Pinky, an impressive woman who has built a multimillion-dollar burger business with no meat. We met at her business in Atlanta, and she has done pop-ups in Oakland and LA but has not built permanent locations in California yet.

It's surprising how my system and body feel lighter when I'm eating plant-based food, yet the burger made me feel fulfilled, just like when I was eating beef. This experience made me fully open to a plant-based diet. I even found a place in my hometown of Oakland, California, with a plant-based taco that is amazing. I now eat mostly vegan meals, replacing meat with hearty, plant-based substitutes most days of the week. My son now jokes that a fast for me is giving up vegetables instead of meat.

One other thing I do to periodically reset my system is the biblical Daniel's Fast, removing meat and sugar for at least twenty-one days, and sometimes doing a fourteen-day cleanse, eating only raw fruits and vegetables. Each time I'm amazed at how good my body feels when I eat more in line with how God created us to eat.

———

Another inspiration for me is Golden State Warriors basketball player Stephen Curry. Steph Curry is a remarkable human being. He is a proud man of faith, a family man, a philanthropist, and an incredible athlete. His dedication and focus despite injury and challenges on and off the court are inspirational.

When he first began playing for the Golden State Warriors, people from all walks of life would approach my son and say he looked like a young Steph Curry. These constant comparisons prompted me to want to meet Steph Curry, which actually happened when my son was eleven! When we met Steph Curry for the first time, the likeness between the two was uncanny. Steph thought so too. In fact, when my son was twenty-five and working as an actor, he was booked for a national commercial for Under Armour, with—you guessed it—Steph Curry.

Curry calls himself a popcorn addict and also has a surprising habit of consuming "empty" carbs before a game. While he normally eats healthy and clean foods, he loads himself up with pasta and popcorn before game time. He said he believes that eating junk takes him back to his childhood days when he used to watch his father play. Luckily, Curry is blessed with a good metabolism and gets away with eating these foods he loves. He's also very driven. He works out five to six days a week then takes one or two days off. He follows different workout plans depending on his focus, including a shooting series, hand-eye coordination series, weighted lunges, and countless other exercises. He also does consistent brain training to improve his decision-making power on the court. His neurocognitive training involves brain drills, special strobe goggles, and many more exercises that you typically wouldn't associate with playing basketball.

Recovery is one of the most important parts of Curry's routine, he says. He performs many stretching exercises like soft-tissue restoration and yoga. He also follows a recovery method that involves sensory deprivation tanks. It's a technique that includes soaking the body in a tank filled with body-temperature water saturated with magnesium and Epsom salts. These minerals help repair body cells, recover muscles, and relax the mind.

I saw a Thrive commercial featuring Steph Curry that had him going into a water pod for his rehab therapy. I thought the treatment looked amazing. Floating in a warm bath, enclosed in a capsule, like a little personal spa—such an incredible concept.

Then, one day I was sitting at a café with a friend and glanced across the street. And behold, I saw the sign that read, "Reboot." Immediately, I said, "That's that pod! I've been looking for a New Thing for this month." So, after lunch, I went across the street to the place. They gave me a tour and explained what the whole experience was. It sounded amazing, and I signed up for three sessions right on the spot. A few days later, I returned for my first session. The place is very calm, and the staff is very helpful. I wore a bathing suit (although it's not required) and climbed into the pod. The water was very warm and full of Epsom salts, which allow you to float on top of the water. They closed the top. Oh my! It was so tranquil, floating in the water. In my meditative state, I thought this must be like what a baby experiences in the womb. When my time was over, I reemerged feeling peaceful, renewed, and restored, and my mind was clear to begin New Things. I left the spa on a natural high, like I was floating on a cloud. After that first visit, I knew I would be back to experience that state again and again.

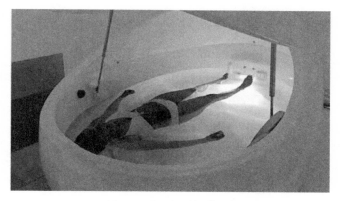

Me experiencing "the float"

For your New Thing this month, find that thing that will reenergize, reinvigorate, and revitalize your mind and body. Whatever new spa thing, new exercise thing, new food thing, or even something from the past that you thought about but didn't try, go for it this month. Above all, your New Thing should fit your physical capabilities and be something that brings you joy. You don't have to become a bodybuilder or have the body of a model; you just have to take care of the body God gave you and celebrate its beauty and capabilities.

EXERCISES:

1. Make a list of physical activities you have participated in with others and enjoyed doing over your lifetime. Make a list of physical activities you would like to do but have never tried.

2. Consider whether your body needs pampering, a cleanse, or a new exercise regimen. How can you accomplish this in a more significant and different way than you have in the past? Is there a health and wellness expo coming up? A wellness retreat or some new exercise or diet plan you have been wanting to try?

3. Do your New Thing for thirty days and document in your journal how you feel mentally and physically. Be sure to add your new regimen to your daily to-do list.

"Write down your vision and make it plain on tablets."
—Habakkuk 2:2

7

IN YOUR OWN
BACKYARD

L ife is a winding journey. People enter your life and leave
your life, and relationships and family dynamics can change
in ways that affect everyone. You can't always foresee the turns
in the road, but you can use the open-mindedness of the 12
New Things Lifestyle to embrace the new and soften the impact.
A change is just another word for a New Thing, and how you
react to it—with more New Things, new ways of thinking and
being—will help you regain your balance, course-correct, or set
you on a path that takes you in a new and different direction.

For instance, when I was growing up in my parents' home,
life was centered around family. The house was always full of
relatives, some even staying with us, and it was always fun.
Cousins, aunts, and uncles from both sides of my family

would come out to visit. My father helped several get into college, or work in the family business, or both. Our home was where everyone gathered, and my parents were the glue that held everyone together. We were like the Huxtables, with two successful parents and a close family unit.

That lasted until the "in-between time," after I graduated from college and before my son was born. That is when everything changed in my family. My parents' business was dissolved, and Mommy suddenly decided to go from Clair Huxtable to Stella gettin' her groove back. She decided to leave the family compound, an 8,800-square-foot estate on close to three acres, to do her own thing. It was final. She had made her mind up. She was done. And at that point, you couldn't have envisioned my parents ever getting back together. These were uncharted waters. It was earth shattering. I was devastated inside, although as a woman, I understood. It was an adjustment for us all. And I mean all—me, my brother, relatives on both sides, and most of our community. My parents were the anchors, and their marriage was the gold standard. On my mom's side, none of her sisters, mother, or grandmothers had gotten a divorce or even legally separated from their spouses. Once again, she was the first. She was the first in her family to graduate from college and the first woman in the long family line to get a divorce.

At this point in life, now that the kids were grown, my mother was looking for her own way, her own space, her own life. Mommy had given everything to the team, the family. And now it was "me time" for her. Even though this was something my mother felt she needed to do, it must have been hard for her to make such a life-changing pivot. Because when she first left, in order to keep her distance, she would resort to being overly mean to my dad to keep space between them. It took some time before they both moved on to having their own lives, sort of.

As time went by, my dad was left living in that big estate on his own. It then dawned on him, "Why am I living in this big ol' house all by myself? I bought it so everyone could be together, and now, no one is here." By this time, I had moved to my first place in San Francisco, and my brother was still in LA with no plans to return to Oakland. So, my parents decided to sell the home we all loved. With everything changing in my world, I decided to change too and look for ventures I could go into. That was when, newly engaged, I moved to Las Vegas.

As I related in previous chapters, the gourmet coffeehouse I started there was a blend of politics, arts, and coffee before Starbucks came to town. After several years in Las Vegas on my own and after breaking off my engagement, change entered my life again in the form of a child. It's funny, but during college, I had told several people that I planned to have a child by a certain age, even if I wasn't married. I knew I wanted to be a mom. In fact, that was the main reason I originally wanted to be married—to have children, my own family.

Now, even though my family had accepted everything I did and were with me all the way, I noticed my mom seemed uneasy with my decision to be a single mom. This may have been a subconscious feeling for her, a remnant of her Southern Baptist roots, even though she was off doing her own thing. She didn't show it openly, but if you knew Mommy, you could tell by her actions it bothered her. The woman who was always there was now suspiciously too busy for things she would normally make herself available for. In the end, my father was the one who went with me to my sonogram appointments when I was flying back and forth from Las Vegas to my doctor visits in California. Mommy was always conveniently preoccupied. I didn't hold it against her, because I was the one who decided to have a child alone. This was my personal decision and responsibility; I did not expect Mommy or anyone to be there. It is just that I noticed that she was not.

Her absence made room for bonding moments between my dad and me, and the appointments gave us a way to become closer. It actually gave me space to learn more about his perspective. I knew hers, but I never really thought about his. During my pregnancy, my dad was all in, especially when he found out I was having a boy. He said, "If that baby comes out looking like a Scott, with light eyes, I am going to take him." Then, when my son, Austin Carrington-Scott, was born, he looked just like my dad, a Scott.

My dad attributes Austin's coming into the world as the change that saved his life. My son gave Daddy purpose again and a reason to go on during a very challenging time in his life. The business, his marriage, the house, and his family were broken up, scattered, gone. When everything was upside down, Austin arrived.

Well, the back-and-forth from Las Vegas to California lasted until a month before my due date. It was time to relocate to Oakland and prepare to give birth and become a mother. By now, I really didn't like Las Vegas as much, so I was fine with coming back to Oakland for what I thought would be a temporary stay. Totally unplanned, I moved in with my dad. This move turned into a two-year stay, which then led to my dad moving in with me for the next twenty-five years.

It was Divine intervention that my dad (also known as *Papou*, which is "grandfather" in Greek) lived with me and my son during his formative years. It allowed for a positive, inspiring male presence to be in the home as a guide for my son. I must admit, I could not have prayed for better parents. My son having his grandfather in his life was crucial to his development as a man. The arrangement gave everyone balance.

My decision to relocate back to Oakland was partially influenced by my son's godmother recruiting me to be the director of the accounting department for the higher education institution where she worked and served as the CEO. The position was designed to be remote, long before the 2020 pandemic, which was perfect for me as a new mom. I worked from home for three days and went into the office twice a week to do administrative tasks, print checks and reports, and meet with students to answer tuition questions. By now, my dad had gone back into working in education but was able to be home on the days I went into the office.

So, this all worked well until one day when my son became ill, and my dad and I both had to go into the office. Luckily, Mommy (also known as *Madear* to her grandchildren) was available to come stay at the house to take care of Austin. Mind you, this was during the time my mom was still exercising her need for space from my dad and any resemblance of that Huxtable relationship we all loved and admired. However, to Mommy's credit, the one thing about her is nursing is in her core. My mother and her mother were both nurses. My mother went to college on a naval nursing scholarship, a full ride to University of Colorado Boulder. Even though she was not practicing at the time, at the end of the day, Mommy is a nurse. I actually often affectionately call her "our Florence Nightingale."

That day, her unconditional love and her exceptional bedside manner led Mommy to come over and nurse my son back to good health. It was at this moment she realized how much she was missing, and she definitely didn't want to be out of this child's life. The walls began coming down, and the grudges and strong disagreements faded. Austin's existence is one of a peacemaker. It was this peace that mended our family's wounds. By Austin opening my mother's heart to love again, this baby boy was the link that brought my parents back together, not as husband and wife, but as friends and family. Between my New Thing as a single mom, and my mom's New Thing as an independent woman, we had a whole new kind of family dynamic. The bottom line is family is family, and this baby course-corrected ours.

We now have family get-togethers again and even travel as a family, all of us. My father goes to events on my mom's side and vice versa. When people see our families together, it's impossible to tell whose side is whose unless you know.

So, this shift in the family dynamic made way years later for us to execute my next New Thing. I was trying to find something local to do with the whole family. Something to do, as they say, "in my own backyard." Because, when you think about it, so many of us take the gems in our home cities for granted. Instead, we travel halfway across the country or the world to attend an event, thinking it's somehow more special because it's far away. Meanwhile, we don't even think about some attractions in our own city or state, or we do not bother visiting until someone from out of town wants to go.

My colleague called me one day with an invitation, as she has done for years. She said, "Would you and your family like to join our camping trip to Yosemite?" I started to decline, but when I thought about it, I realized, *Oh, my goodness! This would be perfect for the "my own backyard" New Thing.*

My mom and son were the first to commit to joining me on the adventure. Then my dad said to count him in, followed by my brother, Kente, and his daughter, my niece, Tyler. We decided to rent a huge SUV to accommodate everyone and, of course, my granddog, Rico. The plan was to have my brother and niece drive up from LA to meet us in the middle of Yosemite. So, the day came, and like the Beverly Hillbillies, we packed up the truck and moved the family to Yosemite for the weekend.

Daddy drove while I copiloted from the front passenger seat. My son was in the backseat with my mom, and in the far back was Rico. Rico slept most of the way, as did Mommy. After leaving the nursing profession to help my dad build one of the top one hundred African American-owned food service businesses in the United States, according to *Black Enterprise* magazine, my mom returned to nursing fifteen years ago. The night before the trip, she had worked the evening shift and was exhausted, coming straight from work to join us for the trip.

As with our past trips, it was all comedy, cutting up, snacks, and road-trip games. Mommy would wake up every time at her turn. I don't know how she does it. Works all night and lives by cat naps during the day. In the midst of playing the game, we began to see the mountains and the rich green trees. The excitement of the adventure was building in all of us.

Finally, we arrived at our cabin and checked in. Mommy and I took the big bedroom while the others found their sleeping quarters in bunks and other rooms.

12 New Things trip to Yosemite with the family

After we were settled, we headed over to an area of cabins where a friend of mine was staying. They had multiple generations of family there at the campsite. Because they have done this for so many years, they were completely prepared. They had all the food, the barbeques, picnic tables for meals, and the fire pit for roasting marshmallows and making s'mores.

That night was so peaceful. The campfire and the brilliant stars in the night sky were so beautiful and romantic; the sky was so clear at night because there were no city lights. Being in the national park under the stars really makes you step back, take a deep breath, and reflect on God's greatness.

The next morning, we were up very early for our hike to see the waterfalls. Getting up the mountain took at least an hour.

We saw lots of squirrels and some deer. It was funny; each time we thought we were near the waterfall, we'd realize it was still much farther up—even though we could see it in front of us. We would make it to one landing, then move on to the next landing to get closer to the waterfall. My dad stopped at one point at the base while Mommy, Kente, Austin, Tyler, and I kept going up.

The family hike to see the waterfall in Yosemite

We finally made it to where the water pooled. It looked beautiful, and I was ready to go in for a dip. I knew the waterfall would be cold because it was from ice melt, so I had brought a swimsuit that was almost like a wetsuit and water shoes to protect my feet from the rocks at the bottom.

Me taking a cool dip at the bottom of the falls

As expected, the water was freezing cold, but to my surprise, refreshing too, especially after our long hike. My son, brother, and niece went farther up, while I was in the water enjoying my New Thing, bathing in the Yosemite waterfall. It was nice to see how Yosemite brought so many people from all over the world together. There were many happy people speaking in different languages enjoying the sights, all of us in such amazement of the majestic mountains and waterfalls.

That night, I was so relaxed, I slept like a baby. The next morning, I awakened to the beautiful sounds of nature, birds chirping, rivers flowing, and crisp mountain air. My son and brother were excited about going fishing, while I took Rico on a long nature walk. After the walk, I spent the day writing and reflecting about how this New Thing touched my spirit. Experiences like this in nature always give me a feeling of a closer connection to God, a oneness with nature.

As the weekend drew to a close, the entire family left Yosemite completely relaxed, inspired, and in awe of this vast expanse of nature right in our own backyard. For you, finding that New Thing in your own backyard could be as simple as finding a museum, park, or attraction that your city or state is famous for but you've never experienced firsthand. Just like doing a New Thing doesn't have to be big, finding a new experience doesn't have to take you far. If it's easily accessible, make the small trip and go for a visit. Better yet, invite your friends or family to create this new memory together.

EXERCISES:

1. Make a list of the places "in your own backyard" you have never visited. Research museums, art galleries, amusement parks, or even a local live theater that has comedy acts or plays. Local parks will often host events like movie nights, local sports games, or even shows like Shakespeare in the Park.

2. Look for seasonal events going on near you. Does your town/city have an iconic or well-known venue or annual big attraction like a renaissance fair, cowboy festival, or rodeo?

3. Make a list of people whom you would like to join you on the journey and start planning your New Thing adventure.

"Life is too short not to try something new."
—Carrie Bradshaw, *And Just Like That*

8

IN A LAND FAR AWAY

Have you ever wondered about the origins of your family? If you were born in the United States, unless you are a Native American, chances are your ancestors were from a faraway place. It was travel that brought our ancestors to this land where they had to create a new life, and it is travel that enables me to search for New Things. For me, travel is always an exhilarating adventure, a chance to immerse myself in new cultures, traditions, and food. The prospect of journeying to a distant land, whether it's a once-in-a-lifetime experience or a familiar routine, always sparks a sense of anticipation and requires careful planning.

Since many of my travels fall around the Christmas season, I am also able to experience the holiday in new settings and experience the nuances of the season in each place. Christmas is celebrated in many ways all over the world, each with its unique customs and traditions, ranging from simple to very elaborate. It's an enchanting time of the year that unites people of all races, ethnicities, and religions, showcasing the beauty of diversity. All around the world, Christmas is a magical time full of big dreams and hopes.

When I was a child, our family tradition was primarily celebrating the holiday at home in Oakland or at one of my parents' hometowns, Houston or Denver, with all the decorations. In my latter years, it included gathering for an annual family portrait.

Our new family Christmas card photo

My brother and me as kids spending Christmas in Texas

One family Christmas tradition that remains to this day is heading to the mountains to ski for a winter wonderland holiday experience. I originally learned how to ski in high school. The beauty of living in California is having sun during all seasons and the convenience of driving a few hours to the mountains and snow in the winter. This New Thing began with my family traveling to Tahoe in December to celebrate my brother's birthday. As the years went by, to change it up, we decided to try skiing in different places. Although not as convenient and a bit pricier because we had to fly, we traveled to Whistler in Canada and Vail in Colorado. Both were exciting new experiences, but Tahoe remained a staple skiing destination where we could easily go.

As an adult, I still tend to travel around Christmas time. I try to take in the Christmas traditions of each place I visit, but I also like to see some of the manmade wonders and unique cultures that each location offers. For instance, on our family trip to Ghana, we got to spend the holiday together but also see and experience a place where some of our ancestors were from. It was the perfect time of year for the weather, and swimming off the Ivory Coast was like floating in bath water. We visited the manmade wonders of the region, like the Kwame Mausoleum, a stunning architectural feat, and Black Star Square, a symbol of Ghana's independence. We also had the unique opportunity to tour the dungeons of the horrific Cape Coast Slave Castle. In this place, African people were brutalized and sold. It is a testament to how strong the ancestors were to survive enslavement and become a vibrant and renewed people.

When visiting a new place, it's not just about seeing the local attractions. If you're visiting a place that your ancestors came from, it's important to embrace the traditions and culture that shaped your family heritage. We learned this firsthand when we visited Ghana. The leaders there hold naming ceremonies to present you with a Ghanaian name. Three generations of my family experienced this beautiful ceremony complete with music, dance, food, and colorful clothing of the village. In this case, our New Thing was embracing a piece of our ancestral past.

The emotional significance of this trip was profound. The experience was one of a lifetime, and fulfilling this celebration together with my family was priceless. When planned in advance, the trip is surprisingly affordable, and we were able to choose from the many different types of packages available. As always, when planning any 12 New Things travel, do your research and check current reviews to find the best travel options for you.

Traveling farther than a road trip doesn't have to break the bank or blow up your credit cards. Since each person has different tastes and likes, don't chase the most popular tourist spots or destinations, but do seek the best location and experiences for you. I have a couple of friends who are avid travelers and have mastered the art of traveling on a budget. Their whole lives, they have scrimped and saved. One of their best strategies is to look for repositioning cruises, which are cruises that take you to a one-way destination where the cruise company begins a new cruise itinerary. This often results in an inexpensive one-way cruise. They then book their trip home using airline miles and do the same for accommodations at the cruise destination for time to explore. It's not for everyone, but they thrived on it as a young family when finances were tight and even now in retirement.

There are also those trips of a lifetime you dream of that may sound expensive, but with some planning ahead and using the resources and opportunities available to you, it can be doable without breaking the bank. One such resource is the use of travel perks. For instance, changing your credit cards to the ones with the most travel perks can set you on the way to a fabulous New Thing adventure. If you are careful, you could use that credit card for purchases and payments for which you would usually use a debit card and begin racking up your points or miles without any extra spending. The key is to remember to pay back the card balance faithfully before the interest is added. Also, just putting away a little cash each week can add up. Find something you buy each week that you don't really need and put that money away. Ultimately, you'll have much more fun using it on your New Thing travel.

———

Not long ago, I was thinking about where I could go on a Christmas ski trip that would be different. Then, I saw an ad depicting a couple of men wearing traditional kandura while skiing in a large, indoor, snowy place in the middle of the United Arab Emirates (UAE). I became fascinated with it. Imagine snow skiing in the desert—who would have thought that was possible? I thought, *This might be a great way to experience a New Thing.*

So, as one of my 12 New Things, I decided to travel to Dubai. Dubai shines as the largest city in the UAE and is a prominent tourism destination, standing at this pinnacle because the people of Dubai are truly big dreamers who can bring feats of world-class luxury shopping, fine dining, and unique attractions to life. They are forward thinkers who use innovation and technology to build modern architecture and manmade landscapes you won't find anywhere else on Earth.

Ski Dubai is one such feat of engineering. This ski facility in the middle of the desert comprises 237,000 square feet of indoor space and is almost a mile long, with manmade snow for skiing, snowboarding, tobogganing, and tubing any time of the year. It's just like a conventional ski resort, except it's indoors. To think that you could build something like this takes a huge imagination. Not to mention it must have been an incredible undertaking and a huge engineering challenge to work out all the logistics throughout this colossal structure, from the refrigeration to the snow-making machines. They opened in 2005, and their business has done better than everyone expected. Just like in the movie *Field of Dreams*, about a farmer who constructs a baseball field in his cornfield, "if you build it, they will come."

I couldn't wait to see and ski inside this manmade wonder. I began my research about what to expect as a woman traveling to Dubai. I learned that everyday attire is acceptable unless you're going to the temple. There, you must dress more con-servatively, and women must wear a headscarf. I also learned Dubai is one of the cleanest, safest places to travel to.

I invited my mom and my childhood friend Ella to join me on this New Thing trip. Ella had traveled to Dubai before, so she was able to fill us in on many details about what to expect. Luckily, I was able to use my reward miles on Alaska Airlines, one of my favorite airlines, and one I partnered with during the Christmas season in 2022 to create a 12 New Things Dream Travel Contest. One 12 New Things participant won a dream trip on Alaska Airlines for two.

For my personal dream trip, I used my Alaska Airlines miles to travel on Emirates Airlines to Dubai. Because I was using reward miles, the trip routed me through Chicago. The day we were leaving was quite hectic. I found myself on the phone at the airport because Chicago was experiencing a massive snowstorm, which was going to make it impossible for me to make my connection. After speaking to an Emirates Airlines attendant and getting nowhere, the call dropped. Then, fortunately, I called Alaska Airlines. At the time, the two airlines were partners and had a great relationship, and the Alaska Airlines agent was able to finish making the change and even secured my upgrade coupon to first class. This meant I would be able to experience Emirates' most exquisite features, like the bar lounge area I had read about.

Arriving in Dubai Airport was like stepping into another world. The airport in itself could be a vast city. Driving into Dubai, I felt like I had stepped into a much cleaner Vegas on steroids. Everything is much bigger, grander, and more opulent. Another big perk was that I used Marriott points for accommodations. We stayed at the JW Marriott on the sixtieth floor. The hotel is made up of two large towers, and the suites are beautiful. There are two pools—perfect for my morning workout—and the views are breathtaking.

On the first day, we headed over to the Mall of the Emirates, where Ski Dubai is located. As we walked into the building, I could hardly believe its size. I checked in and was given my ski gear. Ella and I both skied, and my mom enjoyed the snow activities section, tubing, and playing games in the snow. I went down all of the ski runs several times. There were only a few ski runs in total, but crowds were never a problem because skiers have a designated ski time so that only a small group of people can ski at one time. Everyone, from the staff to the fellow skiers, was very kind, helpful, and pleasant. One of the ski instructors even used my phone to film me going down the mountain. After the skiing fun was done, Mommy,

Indoor skiing and snow fun in Dubai

Ella, and I took the chair lift all the way to the top to a cozy Alpine-themed restaurant, The Avalanche and Ice Café, where we were able to relax and drink hot chocolate.

Then it was time to head over to Burj Khalifa, the tallest building in the world, where Ella and Mommy treated me to a beautiful birthday tea. The elevator was a straight trip to the top with a view that went on forever. You can see the golf courses, the ocean, practically the whole country. We were served tea in elegant teacups. The tea service was first-rate, with trays of finger sandwiches, delicious mini desserts, and aromatic teas. It was fine dining fit for a queen. In Dubai, everything is done on a much grander level. As we sipped our tea and drank in the majestic view, I marveled at the splendor all around us.

We also experienced the more traditional side of Dubai with a fully equipped camel ride followed by a dinner and musical show among the sand dunes. My Dubai trip grew from an inspiration on my 12 New Things list to being a "neat little adventure" and ultimately becoming a life-altering experience that touched every aspect of my life and world outlook.

———

Another fun way to travel is by train; with proper planning, it can be a cost-effective trek. As a family tradition, my son and my father take an annual summer trip by train from California to Colorado, my father's birthplace. They have taken this trip every year since my son was a little over a year old. When my son was in middle school, my father added a New Thing aspect to the annual trek by inviting along my oldest first cousin, Gary, and adding an extra stop to make it a profoundly personal historical journey to where our ancestors lived and attended college. The initial reason for the trip was to deliver a book that my father and his oldest sister, Gary's mom and my Aunt Nan, wrote together about the family legacy and history going back to 1838. The trio went to present the book to the library at Lincoln University, where my aunt and grandmother had attended college.

My dad planned this scenic journey on the California Zephyr train that runs through the Rockies to Denver, Colorado. In Denver, he rented a car, and they drove to Lincoln Hills in Golden, Colorado, to visit the now-historical landmark cabin my great-grandfather built in the 1920s. The family actually named the cabin Zephyr View because of the passenger train that traverses the canyon on its way to and from California.

The next leg of the trip took them to Jefferson City, Missouri, where Lincoln University is located. Lincoln University was founded just after the Civil War by two regiments of Black soldiers who wanted to start a school for emancipated African Americans. My dad, cousin, and son—three generations of men from our family—visited the university, the area where the family lived, and their final resting place. The trip was not just a journey but an enlightening educational experience that deepened my son's understanding of our family's past. It impressed upon him the profound historical significance of Lincoln University and made him familiar with the places his ancestors touched.

———

I have always dreamed big, and travel has always inspired me. After visiting the White House and the Naval Academy one summer with my family when I was ten, I decided my ultimate career goal was to be president of the United States. That trip planted the seed of the dream that led to my passion for politics. Eventually, after my freshman year at UCLA, I would change my business economics major to political science and become a businesswoman immersed in the world of politics. Although I enjoy the world of politics, I decided the role of an elected official was not for me. However, dreaming big led to my role as a presidential appointee to the United States Advisory Committee for Trade Policy and Negotiations.

What does it take to change one's mindset to flip the impossible into "I'm possible"? Often it takes getting out of your everyday routine and visiting someplace new, seeing and experiencing new perspectives and worldviews. By looking beyond the obstacles, you open yourself up to achieve dreams so big, some might consider them wild. So, dream as big as building Dubai and become your ancestors' wildest dreams.

EXERCISES:

1. This month, give yourself the gift of travel. Write out a list of ten places you have never been but want to go to. Or list the places where you can go to discover your ancestry. Then set a budget and start planning your 12 New Things dream trip.

2. Create a vision board of your chosen place or places. You can plan for multiple trips or use this process to help you if you're undecided. As you're looking for images, photos, and inspiration, start dialing in the details of what you want to do there, sights you want to see, and experiences you plan to explore.

3. Now that you have a clear vision, start planning your trip. If you need to save, start saving. If you need to take vacation time, put in for the time off. Whatever you need to do to execute it, do it.

"Enlarge the place of your tent and let the curtains of your habitations be stretched out; do not hold back; lengthen your cords and strengthen your stakes."
—Isaiah 54:2

9

SHAKES ON A SEAPLANE

What is fear, and what are phobias? Where do they come from? Fear is one of our most basic emotions, and it can keep us from achieving any one of our 12 New Things. From the moment we are born, we are thrust from the womb, our comfort zone. We are deluged with activities and experiences that cause us to react by crying, falling quiet, hiding, or staring wide-eyed in shock. Throughout life, our survival instincts respond to new encounters with varied reactions: fight-or-flight, excitement, and everything in between. But why do some people remain unbothered by something like a spider or a sudden noise, whereas someone else may jump and scream?

Some fears in life are valid and are meant to protect us when we're in situations of actual danger. Phobias, on the other hand, I believe, are magnified fears deeply rooted in trauma that enable you to hide. They come from a place of doubt and can sometimes leave us immovable, blocking our blessings. Phobias develop when fears are not addressed, and they become rooted in our core as we struggle to overcome them. Prayer and faith can help you move past both; however, it is not an easy process.

The 12 New Things Lifestyle is my method for facing some of my fears head-on in fun and exciting ways. The thought of trying something you've never done before can cause fear to bubble up, but then going out and actually doing that thing turns anxiety into new adventures and trains our minds to accept that change does not always have to be scary. Sometimes stepping out of our comfort zone and walking by faith can be enjoyable and thrilling. We might find out that on the other side of fear is this beautiful opportunity filled with blessings. Using 12 New Things as a prompt, I encourage you to work on the fear or phobia keeping you from fully embracing all that life has to offer.

My first step to facing fears is to decide whether a particular fear is something I must take head-on to overcome. I ask myself: Why am I letting this fear block me from doing this New Thing? Then, I find a way to be still and listen to God's voice speaking to me. In the stillness, I am calmed and focused on what I need to do to overcome the fear I am facing. Once I am still and centered, I pray to gain the knowledge I need to move forward and succeed. Next, I seek wise counsel, formally and informally; I do my research and ask professional advisors for helpful tips and tools to overcome the issue. I look for something new and fun to do to incorporate as part of my 12 New Things journey.

I clearly have fears, though I don't consider them phobias because they are not debilitating. I would describe myself as "concerned" about heights and flying, especially in little planes, and I do not like snakes. That is to say, I do not have any interest in doing a New Thing that would involve snakes. That would not be fun at all to me. (Although I understand that in some cultures, dreams with snakes mean good fortune and luck. In that case, I might take snakes over heights.)

During one holiday season, my family decided to take a cruise as a New Thing and ring in the New Year at sea. The ship made stops at different ports along the way, and at each stop the cruise company had several authorized excursions to choose from. Most of the activities I had done in some form or another already, and thus, they wouldn't be New Things for me, but there was one that I really wanted to try—one I had always avoided out of fear: zip-lining! After reading everything I could find about it and talking myself into facing this fear, I decided to add zip-lining to my 12 New Things in the New Year. I booked the zip-line tour along with my son, brother, mother, and niece. We were picked up from the ship by our excursion escort, and before I knew it, we were driving deep into beautiful tree-filled mountains. We had to hike a few miles to the top of the zip-line platform, and the whole way up I was begging God to keep us all safe, to let the line hold, to not drop us to our deaths . . . Upon arrival, we were all fitted with harnesses and given a set of safety instructions, which only made my heart thud faster in my chest. All helmeted and harnessed up, I stepped to the edge of the platform . . . and the next thing I knew, I was flying through the air. It was the most incredible feeling. I soared over the very same road we came in on. After praying to God for safety during the entire excursion, ironically, in the end, I found myself thanking the Lord in gratitude for the joy of this family trip. Such an amazing experience.

Soaring over the road on a zip line

Travel has a way of putting you in new situations, sometimes out of your control, and pushing you to face your fears in the process. Flying has always been uneventful for me, even though I often travel on jet planes all over the world. When we planned our Dubai trip, we also included a stop in the Maldives on our trip home. I had always wanted to go to the Maldives, but by itself, it is a very long trip from California. From Dubai, the flight is much easier, and so it was perfect to use my additional reward points.

During the planning process, I realized we would have to take a small plane to get to the Maldives. This was an issue with me because I had not liked or flown in little planes since I was a teenager. My parents were co-owners of an airline, Pacific Air, the precursor to Southwest in California. Like Southwest, Pacific Air started as a commuter airline with routes from Oakland to Reno and Long Beach. One time, when I was in high school, I traveled with my dad, uncle, cousin, and brother to Reno. Now, flights to Reno are usually bad, but this time, the ride was even rougher than usual, and at one point, the plane suddenly dropped down in mid-flight. It was the most horrific flying experience, and I've been terrified of small planes ever since. Even with that bad experience, my desire to see the Maldives outweighed my fear of flying in a small plane. I decided I wanted to go to the Maldives, and this was the only way to get there.

The first leg of our journey was four hours from Dubai on a regular airplane. On arrival to the Maldives and Velana International Airport, it was hot and very humid, and it didn't seem like there was any air-conditioning. I couldn't wait to get to the resort, but we first had to go through the long line at customs. There were so many people! It was very crowded, and we were only allowed to go through one by one.

When we finally checked in for our next flight, I learned that not only would the next leg of our journey be on a little plane, but that it was a propeller plane, and even worse, it was an eight-seat seaplane! Meaning we were going to take off and land in the water. Before I can process my fear enough to protest, it's time to board. I'm busy talking to myself as we are led outside. Then I see it, a little plane floating in the water tied up to the dock. I'm remembering all of the reviews that I found in my research about the pilots flying barefoot and having a big knife in case they end up having to swim. I read that it's hot and noisy and a bit like how I would imagine a helicopter. (Although, of course, I've never been in one of those.)

Still in my head praying and trying to keep it all together, I barely notice the motion as we climb up the ladder into this little plane. As we find our seats, I notice every seat is taken. So, here we are, eight people and luggage all packed into this tiny plane bobbing in the water. It was tight. We were practically sitting with the pilot in the cockpit! It was like the whole plane was the cockpit with wings with everyone all squeezed together. Then I hear the propellers starting up. They are loud! The little plane began to move from the airport dock. It gathered speed farther out into the water, and we lifted off from the surface!

This is where the shakes come in—it's so shaky, so hot, so humid, and so loud in that little plane. As I peer out the window, I gradually see the ocean drop farther and farther away. I thought "seaplane" meant we would stay low to the water, but no, the small plane was going up 10,000 feet or more into the sky. There we are, high over the Indian Ocean. All I can see out the window are water and spots of land, which are the Maldives islands. I immediately start praying and listening to God's silent voice speaking to me. And I thought the trip would be maybe ten minutes; it was more like forty-five. Through my anxiety, I began to feel a breakthrough, then I could start to appreciate the little clusters of land below, each its own resort.

Finally, we landed in the water. The landing was surprisingly soft; it was actually really cool to land gracefully on the Indian Ocean. Upon landing, any concern in my mind just melted away. When we arrived at the dock, we were greeted with pineapple drinks served in coconut shells and escorted to check-in. Then we were escorted by golf cart to our rooms, stylish over-water villas with the Indian Ocean as the backdrop.

The next four nights were some of the most relaxing I've ever known, spent in the beautiful Maldives, where you could jump from your room right into the Indian Ocean and swim with schools of tropical fish. I found a happy place where all I felt was peace. This resort was such a great, secluded environment for clearing my mind and unwinding. It was also the perfect place to write and let my creative juices flow. My thoughts flowed onto the pages in between lying in the mesh hammock overhanging the bright blue water, swimming with the manta rays, and biking around the island. The food was amazing, including fresh seafood and marvelous brunches with egg scrambles topped with crème, caviar, and edible flowers. We enjoyed craft cocktails at happy hour with music, a barbeque luau, magical sunsets, and chauffeur-driven carts that pick you up for dinner. We all had the best massages at the spa and then went into The Big Blue, the gigantic saltwater Jacuzzi filled with fresh ocean water.

In the evening in the dark of night, you could see nothing but a sea of stars. Astronomers love the Maldives because you are able to see so much more in the night sky. There is a very mesmerizing effect at night with creatures that glow in the sand. I slept well every night listening to the calming ocean waves lapping at the back deck of the villa. In every room, they provide snorkel gear and a life jacket to enjoy the ocean from your personal balcony. Everyday activities include snorkeling and biking around the island. Using their equipment, I spent my time enjoying wonderful days in the ocean, swimming around the reefs and gazing at the many different types of tropical fish. My reoccurring thought was, *I will definitely come back to let my creative mind loose again someday.*

To experience this awesome New Thing adventure, I had to face and overcome one of my oldest fears. Is there something you need to overcome to do one of your New Things? If so, you're not alone; there are many fears and phobias that hold people back, everything from the fear of heights, flying, water, or fire to the fear of spiders, snakes, and creepy crawlies. There is even such a thing as a fear of people wearing socks with sandals. The latter makes it obvious that sometimes we have silly or irrational fears where you just have to say, "Let it go!" I have found life is much more fulfilling when we step out on faith and overcome our fears to get to the other side where our blessings and joy reside.

Taking time to break down a fear to trace back where it came from can help you to face it, allowing you to work through it. There are those traumas we may experience as a child, like a bad experience with a dog or natural incidents like fire, lightning, or earthquakes. Overcoming a childhood trauma can sometimes require help. One friend had a daughter who was afraid of fire because they had a grease fire in the kitchen when she was very little. The fear was so great that she would not let anyone even light the fireplace. Her father was able to work through the fear with her, beginning with having her light little fires in the fireplace and gradually moving to larger fires with logs.

If you're struggling with a deep-rooted fear or trauma, there's no shame in seeking help from someone who loves you or a professional to be your guide through the process. How do you know if you can overcome fear on your own or need the help of a therapist? If you attempt to face a fear and find yourself filled with greater anxiety and fear a week later, you might need professional guidance to find the right approach. Daunting as it may seem, working through fear step by step, in a safe and methodical way, can open you up to all sorts of new and wonderful things.

The fears you need to work on are the ones that are keeping you from the New Things you want to achieve. If it's a silly fear or irrational fear that's keeping you from trying a New Thing like travel, going to a new restaurant, competing in a sport, being around people, or enjoying something you have wanted to do, find a way through it. Take baby steps to prepare yourself to at least try. Irrational fears are those you place in your own way when no actual threat exists—brought on by your own imaginings, letting the negative thoughts build in your mind. Just ask yourself, what do you have to lose? A fear you have kept deep inside since you were a child may not even be a real fear, and once faced as an adult, may be nothing at all.

EXERCISES:

1. Make a list of your fears and things that make you uncomfortable.

2. Identify the ones holding you back from accomplishing your goals or having fun.

3. Start with one fear and write the steps you would take to overcome it. For example, if your fear of heights is keeping you from zip-lining even though you've always dreamed of seeing the Amazon rainforest from that angle, search for activities in your area that would expose you to mild heights, such as indoor rock climbing. Or if you're afraid of water because you never learned to swim, you could search for a local pool or YMCA with adult swim classes.

4. Take the steps to overcoming your fear and be sure to reward yourself when you have accomplished it.

"Be strong and courageous. Do not fear or be in dread of them, for it is the Lord your God who goes with you. He will not leave you or forsake you."
—Deuteronomy 3:16

10

THE GIFT OF GIVING

Another way you can experience one or even two of your 12 New Things is through random acts of kindness or the gift of giving. There are many ways you can create a platform for giving, and it doesn't always have to involve spending a lot of money. Your gift could be sharing a skill you possess, volunteering your time, or giving away something you no longer need or have too much of. In this chapter we'll talk about a few ways you can do this and how giving through random acts of kindness can lead you to receive blessings in many unforeseen and unimaginable ways.

Acts of generosity benefit not just the recipient but the giver as well. These acts give us great happiness, make us feel good, lower our blood pressure, and lengthen our life. We may also experience better mental health. Additionally, through some avenues of giving, our social connections increase.

Not to mention, giving is contagious—who knows what positive chain of events your random act of kindness can kindle? Sometimes when you are giving, it can reintroduce friends and family to the importance of generosity. If others learn you are giving to a charity, it can be an incentive for them to also give. By giving to a non-profit or creating one to become a vehicle of giving, you may well be helping to remind friends and family of causes they themselves are passionate about and would like to support. Charitable giving allows you to pass along opportunities to those needing guidance, support, and a chance to regain their independence, health, and happiness. Oftentimes, your donation is a way of reinvesting back into the community and organizations that have positively impacted your life. Or you can "pay it forward" and give your time or money to a cause that you have not been associated with in the past.

Remember, "giving back" and "paying it forward" does not have to mean that you're donating monetarily. You can give your time, advising and looking out for others without condition. Instead of expecting anything in return, you're doing it as a gesture of gratitude toward those who have helped you in the past or a gesture of unconditional support for someone you've never met. For instance, you can offer your skills to help someone who doesn't have those skills or needs your support to level up. Encourage or uplift someone to step out of their comfort zone and support their New

Thing journey. Then, the person you're helping will now have the tools to help others in the future, and that's how the chain of giving goes.

Another totally free way to give is simply by writing someone an unexpected, kind note to bring cheer to their day. In our electronic world, sometimes mailing a handwritten card to someone you haven't been in contact with in a long while touches them much more than a text or an email. Your New Thing could be to send a thank-you note to a different essential worker each month. Or it could be to link up with a senior in your community, pick them up, and take them to the market or help them with another activity in their day. Or it could be to go through your house and donate the duplicates and things you no longer use. This last kind act will not only help someone else but also help to clear your clutter and make breathing room for more New Things.

All through my life, from an early age, I experienced how my family gave in a variety of ways. Because our extended family was so large, there was always a lot of personal giving but also through church, school, and community. During the holidays and other occasions, my family's church, Joshua Christian Church, led by my mother's brother and his wife, Pastors Donald and Lesley Scurry, would have events to feed people in the community. Mommy and the other women in leadership in the church would cook, while my cousins and I would be on the serving line.

When my son was old enough, I made sure to get him involved early by joining my friends' family church, led by Pastor Zac and Dr. Donna Carey, at True Vine Ministries and their S.A.V.E. our community rallies. True Vine, with its large number of young Black men in the church, was the perfect place for my son to grow in the Lord. Involving my son early was important to me because when my brother and I were growing up, my mom had done the same for us.

We learned the importance of community early in life. My parents both worked at some point in their careers in education. I fondly remember my mother co-leading the middle school students in the Black Student Union (BSU) in Oakland public schools to organize an annual trip to Southern California. She would help manage the student-led fundraisers that paid for the bus, theme park tickets, and meals. On the day of the trip, we would board the buses very early in the morning to make the 342-mile drive to Magic Mountain theme park. The trip was over five hours, but no one cared because it was such a fun getaway from Oakland and Northern California. My father was always involved as well, giving of his time as a parent chaperone and supporting my mother.

Although he helped out with my mother's projects, my father was mainly involved on the political side, as the co-founder of the Niagara Democratic Club, a political organizing group that helped elect the first wave of Black elected officials in Oakland in the 1970s and '80s. When I was old enough, I would tag along with my dad to the weekend Niagara meetings. The Niagara meetings engaged people early on, getting people involved to support candidates. The Oakland Niagara Movement was established in 1973, but the Niagara Movement itself dates back to the early twentieth century, when a group of prominent Black intellectuals led by W. E. B. Du Bois and William Monroe Trotter came together to fight for civil and political rights for African Americans. Being on the forefront of these organizations provided my parents with platforms that allowed them to each give back to the community and model this generosity of spirit for their children.

If you're looking for a way to give to your community, organizations like those mentioned are a great starting point. You might look for an organization that supports people during the holidays or somehow otherwise makes a positive impact on the lives of others. For instance, when my family moved our Thanksgiving celebrations to Houston to be with Grandmother, who had reached her hundreds, we looked for a way to give to the community there. The first time we spent Thanksgiving in Houston, since we were away from home, we went to a "feed the community" event hosted by Texas Congresswoman Sheila Jackson Lee and some other local leaders, which was the perfect opportunity for us to volunteer away from home. Before our big family dinner, we all pitched in serving the community with a well-organized Thanksgiving feast.

The holidays are a natural time of giving, but that's not to say you can't give in other seasons or (seemingly) at random. I have personally started to delve into finding different random ways of giving, such as leaving an additional sizable tip for the server after noticing their exceptional service or overhearing a need. I've also anonymously paid the rent of low-income housing residents and bought an unsheltered stranger a meal or paid for the meal of the next customer or two behind me in line. The idea of "paying it forward" like this isn't a new one, but the idea of doing it with intentionality in a concentrated effort for a solid month is. Why be so systematic about something that is meant to be random by nature? Because only the deeds and their recipients are meant to be random, not the act of giving itself. This challenge teaches the value of being purposeful and intentional.

It's biblical: "As ye sow, so shall ye reap." In other words, extending goodness out into the world will invite goodness to return to us. It's a universal principle. Acts of positivity can be transformative for the giver and the recipient. Thus, the more giving becomes a practice in our lives, rather than an occasional or seasonal good deed, the more we can create opportunities for ourselves while also helping to make the world a better place.

With giving both monetarily and of the self, be mindful of giving according to the expansion you want to see in your life. Tithing is a great way to provide a basis on what to give.

Tithing in the Bible refers to giving 10 percent of your annual earnings, productions, or possessions. In the Old Testament, Abraham and Jacob offer a "tithe" to God in Genesis 14 and 28. The beauty I have found with tithing is giving at least 10 percent yields more than my gift. It is important to measure with your heart, meaning be a cheerful giver, not methodical, because the capacity of the blessings is based on your heart. If a person gives their last dollar as a testament of faith, that could yield more than someone with millions in the bank giving $100K. In giving, the size of the gift does not matter as much as the size of the sacrifice.

Honestly, I cannot tell you how expansion through giving works; I just know that it does. As a young entrepreneur, there were several times I gave away the last five dollars I found hidden in my purse as my tithe. That gift was way more than 10 percent of what I had at the time. I gave with joy that I had something to give during the offering. I was cheerful and grateful too. I recall one time I gave in this fashion only to receive word a few days later that the loan for my home was approved. Like I said, I cannot tell you how. I can only speak to countless examples of it working. Cheerfully giving really works to grow the joy in your life, and what a great way to make your giving a part of your 12 New Things journey by doing random acts of kindness along the way.

If you're curious about how it's working in your own life, this is also a good thing to document in your journal. Doing so will help you correlate each of your acts of kindness in the short term and through extrapolation over time in the long term—not for the recipient of your generosity, but for yourself. Is there a way to know how that big tip helped that waitress? Probably not. But is there a way, through journaling and thoughtful reflection, to see how that charitable gesture affected us and to connect it with how we conduct our lives going forward? Absolutely. We can discover how releasing things that we hold on to but do not necessarily need helps us grow as individuals.

Another way to give throughout the year as part of a 12 New Things journey is to plan welcoming parties for new neighbors to your block, apartment complex, or condo building. Become your community's own "welcome wagon," which is the name of an actual marketing business that welcomes new movers with coupons and advertisements from local establishments to show them what's in town. The company started in Memphis, Tennessee, in 1928. In the early days, they hired women who were friendly and knowledgeable to visit newcomers and, over coffee, fill them in on their new city. They were inspired by old folk stories of wagons meeting travelers going west to offer food and water, and their modern-day efforts still embody that old spirit of hospitality.

So, one of your 12 New Things in the giving category could be to welcome a new neighbor. If you have learned anything about them beforehand, you could personalize your welcome gift or just present them with something neutral like cookies, a plant, or some other item that might be helpful in their new home.

You can do random acts of kindness any time, or you could schedule it for your New Thing in a given month. You could pick February because Random Acts of Kindness Day is February 17th, a tradition that started in New Zealand. Or you could pick December, because the Christmas holiday season is always a good time to give. There are all sorts of opportunities to give presents to the church, fire station, local news station, or any of the other advertised drives in your community. Or you could come up with your own thing. For example, during the 12 days of Christmas, you could buy little tins and put some money in each one, different denominations ranging from $50 to $100. Then write little notes with a line of Scripture and wrap it around the bills in each tin. Throughout the day, randomly give them out as the opportunity arises.

Whereas charitable giving and random acts of kindness are more of an individual thing, "philanthropy" refers to more long-term, strategic giving. It often involves multiple gifts to help people over a specific amount of time. While charitable giving is focused on providing immediate relief to people and is often driven by emotions, philanthropy is focused on helping people and solving their problems over the long term, usually by corporations. By being involved in or supporting a non-profit or other type of entity that gives back, you will be able to help them continue their good work on a large scale. Since I am an alumna of UCLA, I thought the Arthur Ashe Legacy at UCLA was a good way for me to give. I have always admired Arthur Ashe for his accomplishments, contributions to the world of sports, and AIDS awareness. He started playing tennis at six years old. He was the first Black player selected to the United States Davis Cup Team and the only Black male to ever win the singles title at Wimbledon, the US Open, and the Australian Open. The Arthur Ashe Legacy at UCLA is dedicated to honoring Ashe's many achievements by supporting today's students and scholars who exemplify his values. They organize events that celebrate his impact and showcase the lessons we can learn from his legacy today.

As we discussed earlier, giving doesn't always have to be monetary; you can use your skills or knowledge to serve others in important moments. One of my 12 New Things activities turned into an unexpected act of kindness in a crazy way. Some months after I had experienced zip-lining for the first time, I presented at a women's conference in Tulum, Mexico. As part of the trip, the organizer scheduled the presenters for a post-event activity: zip-lining with cave diving in the cenotes. The cave-diving part was interesting to me, but I really didn't want to zip-line again. I thought to myself, *Once we get out there, I can do something else.* However, on the way, I found out a few of the ladies in our group didn't know how to swim. They thought they would make this event one of their New

Things, and they felt safe because they would be wearing life jackets. But in my mind, I began to worry about them. I applaud them for wanting to do this New Thing, but with everything the excursion involved, it seemed to me they were putting themselves in unsafe conditions! Much to everyone's surprise, including the organizer's, cave diving in the cenotes entailed diving into pools of water at the bottom of the caves.

Now, I have helped many people overcome their fear of swimming and have helped many learn how to swim or at least get comfortable in the water. But that's in a pool or in the calm waters of a local beach. Not in an underground pool at the bottom of a cave that you can only reach by zip line! The lifeguard in me led me to commit to joining the activity to at least go ahead of our team to make sure the landscape and the non-swimmers were all safe.

So, we're all out there. The guides fit us with the harnesses, helmets, and life vests. We go through the first part of the zip-lining, then we arrive at the cave-diving part. As the non-swimmers realize what they are about to encounter, they begin to get nervous. The guides, due to the language barrier, do not understand that some in our group do not know how to swim! Everyone has signed their life away to this adventure, and the guides have no clue as to their skill level.

My role immediately shifts from keynote speaker to swim angel, helping my colleagues overcome their fear of water and navigate the logistics of dropping into the cave from the top of a well or zip line into waters at least fifty feet deep. I decided to go first to get the lay of the land and to position myself on the other side to help them. I rappelled down into the cave. One by one the others followed. Although they were wearing life jackets, they still had to swim to the other side to go out. And if they turned over in their life jackets and their faces ended up in the water, they could still have drowned. And what if one of them slipped out of the life jacket? I started to question what on earth I had gotten myself into . . .

Cave diving in the cenotes

Here I am down in the belly of the cenote doing superhero stuff, filled with anxiety, and all the while trying to help keep folks alive! Finally, everyone is safely out of the cave, and now we have to get back. But the only way to get back is to walk through the rainforest and then zip-line down the hill—into water again!

The guide instructed that at the end of the line, you just pull yourself out with the ropes. I decided to go first to meet everyone at the end and make sure the course was safe. Good thing I did, because at the end of the course, the ropes were actually down underneath the water. How on earth is someone who is afraid of the water going to go down into the water to find the ropes? I found one rope when I got down there and had to figure out that you need to find both ropes to really pull yourself out easily. Now while pulling myself up by these ropes, I had to help guide several of the ladies through the waters and safely to shore. By the grace of God, we all made it to the other side, and everyone felt accomplished that they overcame their fear and did a New Thing, including me. Cave diving was a new experience, but as I said before, it really turned out to be one of my acts of kindness as I became the swim angel.

This whole experience makes me want to preface the 12 New Things Lifestyle with this important advice: Be sure you have at least the basic skill set associated with the New Thing you're looking to do!

Opportunities for acts of kindness often come at you this way, not as something planned, but as a decision you make in the moment to do the caring, generous thing. So, as you go through your month of giving, in addition to intentionally looking for outlets for donating, volunteering, or gifting, be open to moments and situations where you can choose to do a kind act. That too is the beauty of random acts of giving.

EXERCISES:

1. Review what charitable acts you already do.

2. Review your financial giving and decide on a percentage you feel comfortable and happy giving.

3. Make a list of charitable entities you would like to support. What connection do you feel to them or their acts?

4. Make a list of non-monetary things you are able to do to help and benefit others.

5. Go through your house and find things you no longer use or have duplicates of and donate them.

6. Decide on your random act of kindness this month and begin giving.

THE GIFT OF GIVING

"Each of you should give what you have decided in your heart to give, not reluctantly or under compulsion, for God loves a cheerful giver. And God is able to bless you abundantly, so that in all things at all times, having all that you need, you will abound in every good work."

—2 Corinthians 9:7-8

11

LOVE WILL FIND A WAY

Love is patient and kind, love does not envy,
love does not parade itself, it is not puffed up.

—1 Corinthians 13:4

I t takes a long time to get to know someone's true inner self to see if they really are the one to be there through thick and thin, good, bad, happy, and sad because relationships take work, understanding, and mutual respect. Using the 12 New Things Lifestyle will help you to gauge, test, and strengthen the love you have or the one you are trying to realize as a true love.

Before we set out to seek love or improve the one we've already found, we need to know ourselves. That is the essence of the 12 New Things Lifestyle—doing New Things to get to know yourself better and become your best self to be compatible with others. How do you accomplish that?

It all begins with you. Do you know yourself? What do you like about yourself? What aspects of yourself do you want to change? You'll find the answers to these questions when you spend quality time with yourself. It is a form of self-care and love. In the 12 New Things Lifestyle, we call this "a date with Self."

Spending time with yourself also allows time to focus on making yourself happy. Because if you don't have internal happiness, you cannot be satisfied with external partners. Once you find love of Self, the others follow. Put in terms of 12 New Things, a New Thing you can start is a self-care routine, setting aside "me time" to have a date with yourself.

Fridays are my "me time" (which my family calls "Shonda time"), and I often use Fridays to do something new with just me. To get started, I begin by thinking of fun things I want to do. I always make it an exciting and joyful experience. New Things that I have done during my "Shonda time" are a winemaking class, a sushi-making class, a night away in Monterey, and a drive to the beach to sit by the ocean and write. The winemaking class not only taught us about how wine is processed in oak barrels or stainless steel, but we also learned how to blend wines. We even got to try our hand at making our own blend, and after several tries and sipping lots of wine, you determine which blends are your top three and then select one special blend of your own. The one I created was based on the coincidence that I created the same formula twice. I figured that was a sign. I went with that blend and named it Shonda Love. Now I have my own blend and label with a name that reminds me of the purpose of that evening: loving oneself and showing oneself love.

Cooking classes are ideal for 12 New Things activities. In my search for something new, I found an exciting sushi-making class happening on a Friday. I signed up immediately with enthusiasm, one, because I like sushi, and two, I am always on the lookout for something new to do. The class was the perfect mix of date-nighters, groups of friends, and me as part of my 12 New Things journey. It was an evening of learning about, rolling, and slicing sushi, while at the same time meeting new people and enjoying the artistry of making beautiful sushi rolls.

Google searches, Airbnb experiences, and friends' recommendations have been great resources for me to find new adventures and dates to take myself on. I usually choose some activity that I think I will like but have never experienced before. Think of things you love to do and, even if you'd typically share the experience with a friend or family member, consider taking yourself out for a special date to deepen your connection with Self.

In this age of technology, there are more ways to connect with people than ever before. Traditionally, you would meet a potential new match through friends, community settings like school or church, or an interested family member setting you up. Now, dating apps have made it easier than ever for people to connect. If you are single, I recommend using the 12 New Things journey to find creative ways to meet people you might be compatible with. I was once invited to participate on a TV show on dating, and I used it as part of the 12 New Things adventure for the month. I used the process to find tools to help me heal my heart and identify new ways to engage when dating. In my interview, I realized that I lead with my head, and the recommendation was for me to lead with my heart. These experiences and new perspectives have opened me up to meet new people and learn more about myself.

As a single mom, dating can often be a bit challenging. It was that way for me because I was not only thinking about what was best for me, I was always thinking about my son, too. It took a blind date set up by mutual friends to bring a deep love into my life. His friend did not know me, and my friend did not personally know him. Our friends just knew we were both incredible, kind, exceptional people. Based on my friend's description of me, his friend felt I would be a great connection. Neither of us were in the habit of calling people we didn't know, yet this time we both did something new and different. Our mutual friends asked if I would give him my phone number, and my ultra-private self agreed. After a few weeks, I received a call from my friend, who said, "He has your phone number, so answer when he calls, because he will call you." Sure enough, a few days later, I received the call.

After another few calls, we both did something else new: We agreed to meet in person. This would be our first meeting, and we didn't realize at this time that our friends who set us up had not met either of us in person. So, both acting on faith and the trust we put in our close friends, we decided to meet at a lovely café in Santa Monica. He lived on the East Coast, and I lived on the West Coast but in Northern California. Los Angeles was on my coast, but it was still neutral ground for us. Because Los Angeles has always been one of my favorite cities in the United States, and attending UCLA made me love it even more, I was happy to meet there.

From that meeting forward, we developed a lifelong friendship and an undying love filled with mutual respect. One that is more unconditional than I have experienced outside of my family. Stepping out on faith for this love connection has brought something much more beyond the light meal we enjoyed that day in that Santa Monica café. There have been walks on the beach, prayers for one another, birthday celebrations, sporting events, and not one but two Hall of Fame celebrations for both me and him. I cannot imagine life without him in it, and it still amazes us to this day that a call to a stranger and a blind date brought us this everlasting special love connection beyond either of our own understandings.

Before his mother passed, she and I had become pen pals, celebrating our birthdays with greeting cards and quotes from our favorite Scriptures. He blessed my family, and I blessed his. Our chance connection linked us together because we did not let fear block our blessings. We decided to do something new and different.

It took the pandemic for my brother to meet the love of his life. This circumstance made him do something new and different to get to the blessings on the other side. Due to the shelter-in-place order, his love refused to meet in person. They dated for months remotely, while living in the same city. They had traveled in the same circle for years but never connected until right before the pandemic, on a cruise, where they exchanged numbers. Then the pandemic happened. It took the stillness of quarantine to give them both time to stop moving and cherish moments on Zoom to truly connect. Both of them had adult children, so they had that in common. During their FaceTime calls, they were able to spend time together and learn about one another. Building a relationship through communication without physical contact gave their love room to blossom.

Committing to a 12 New Things Lifestyle is committing to not letting fear block your blessings. It is committing to opening your mind and heart to New Things. New Things mean new adventures, new opportunities, and new people too. It has been said that if you want to see a different outcome, you have to start by doing something new.

The 12 New Things mindset is what birthed me, both physically and spiritually. My parents met long before I was born, when my mother decided to go on a hayride with her college roommate and (by Divine intervention) so was my father, with his date. According to my father, when he saw the beautiful, café-latte-colored petite collegiate, he was smitten. Since he was a gentleman and he was on a date, he did not ask my mother for her phone number that day. But not having that information did not stop him. He found out her name and that she was in nursing school at the University of Colorado on a naval scholarship. That was just enough information for him to act on and do something new.

Later that month, my father went on a mission to the university to find the beautiful café latte queen named Frazier. Surely there was only one woman named Frazier on campus. And as luck would have it, my mother was the only Frazier on campus and one of only two Black women in the nursing program. My dad had no problem finding his love. When he arrived, six-feet-two-inches tall, handsome, with dreamy blue-green eyes, she gladly accepted his offer to go on their first date.

Doing something new, in my parents' case, led to them finding each other and building a family, a community, and a successful, prominent business in the 1980s. Their willingness to try New Things brought them to a place where they hired hundreds of people and positively impacted the lives of thousands.

So, when you find that new intimate relationship or want to become closer to your special someone, it does take work. With the 12 New Things Lifestyle, you can make the work fun by committing together to doing New Things each month. Doing so will bring you out of your comfort zone, expand your adventures, and push you to grow personally, and at the same time, it will grow your bond.

EXERCISES:

1. Make a list of New Things to do on a date with yourself. After the date, journal about your new experience and what you learned about yourself from it.

2. If you're in a new relationship, make a list of New Things to do together so you can interact and get to know one another better. Journal about your experience and how the other person made you feel; this will help you decide the future of the relationship.

3. If you're in a longtime relationship, make a list of New Things to do with your partner to renew your relationship and have fun. You can find new ways to enjoy activities you've both liked in the past, have one partner introduce the other to a favorite hobby, or

try something that's new to both of you. Make this a once-a-month date night New Thing.

"And let us consider how we may spur one another on toward love and good deeds, not giving up meeting together, as some are in the habit of doing, but encouraging one another—and all the more as you see the Day approaching."

—Hebrews 10:24-25

12

IT'S A FAMILY AFFAIR

If there is one thing in life that epitomizes the drama of a sudden change, it's the arrival of a newborn child. Even the best-behaved children demand our attention, scramble our ability to think, and show us just how upside down we must have made our parents' world when we were young. It's no wonder comedienne (and mother of two) Wanda Sykes likes to joke, with the slyest of smiles, "Oh yeah. But they are worth it." To navigate through the unknown waters of new parenthood, one must call on the people around them. We can't take somebody's preorganized plan and believe it's the way, because no two family dynamics are the same. Each family unit is different—one parent, two parents, grandparents, uncles, aunts—and everyone looks at other families and thinks they know what they are doing and have it made. They don't. Everyone struggles, even when they have help from family.

Grandparents are a huge part of raising kids in many households. In 2019, an AARP survey revealed that 11 percent of grandparents live in the same household as their grandchildren and babysit, and 5 percent of grandparents provide their grandchildren's primary care.[2] If you care for small children, grandchildren, or elderly parents, you may think that you don't have time for New Things. But adopting the 12 New Things Lifestyle can help keep you healthy and boost your well-being. It is paramount to do at least one New Thing each month, something new and different that takes you out of the caregiver mode.

And you must not feel any guilt or remorse for taking time for yourself. Where there is a will, there is a way. Someone in your family circle, friends, or even an outside caregiver who has been highly recommended can take on your duties for an hour, a day, or even a week. If you don't have the village of family, then your next New Thing must be to seek out, interview, background check, and do a trial run with someone you can trust to care for your loved ones when you need a break. Even in a two-parent family, one usually takes on the majority of the caregiving to alleviate the other, who may provide the bulk of the household income. You must build your own village.

---

2   AARP, "New AARP Research on Grandparents Busts Stereotypes on Attitudes, Employment, Finances and Lifestyle," April 8, 2019, https://press.aarp.org/2019-4-9-new-aarp-research-on-grandparents-busts-stereotypes-on-attitudes-employment-finances-and-lifestyle.

You may be the parent always running around with small children and taking care of a busy home while also doing the shopping, running errands, and looking out for elderly parents who are ailing but still living on their own. Still, it's important to take time for yourself at least once a month—even more so because so many are relying on you and making constant demands on your time—and the 12 New Things Lifestyle can give you that nudge to do so. There are so many families today with three or more generations under one roof. When there are both young and old and just more people in the house, there is always the one person who is trying to manage them all. If the one who is doing all the caregiving is not mindful of their own needs, they'll end up like my friend who passed out in her kitchen only to wake up alone realizing she needed a break. Most importantly, she found that planning to properly care for yourself is a must. The 12 New Things Lifestyle gives you a template and a prompt to do just that.

If you are the other parent, the one who is the major earner, then your next New Thing is to help find that caregiver, so your spouse/partner can take care of their mental, physical, and spiritual needs. This will not only help rejuvenate the spouse but also alleviate any stress in your family dynamic, leading to a more unified partnership and family unit.

Everyone benefits from the 12 New Things Lifestyle, even your children. Start them with their own New Thing while they are young. Show them how to plan a New Thing each month. Your elderly parents will also benefit from adding the 12 New Things Lifestyle to enhance their golden years. Whether your elderly parent lives with you, is still on their own, or lives in a senior living community, 12 New Things can enhance their lives by giving them New Things to keep their mind, body, and spirit thriving. No matter how old someone is, the benefits of challenging oneself to do at least one New Thing each month will give a greater quality of life.

When I decided to become a mom, I was a very independent, type A, unmarried woman with my own business. I prayed for a son, and God blessed me with one. I felt I had accomplished most of the things on my list of goals at the time, and I welcomed motherhood. When the due date finally came, I went to the hospital with a whole entourage. As I was going into labor with my legs propped up preparing to push, I suddenly looked up and wondered, *Why do I have all these people in the room with me?* I had never thought about all that they were about to experience and see! My son's godmother was filming, and she got the best footage. She got everything—and I mean, everything. When I first looked at the video, I thought once again, *Oh, my goodness, why'd I have all these people in the room? And they were seeing all of this!* So, I didn't even watch the whole video until my son's eighteenth birthday. We went up to visit him at college at California State University, Sacramento, and I had videos from his birth to the first seven years put on a CD for him to have. He was such a big, beautiful baby. He looked like a butterball turkey when he came out, eight pounds, four ounces, and twenty-one and a half inches long. What joy he brought to all our lives. After much consideration and prayer, I decided to name him Austin Carrington-Scott.

From the moment I found out I was pregnant my life began to gradually change. My plan was to have my child in the Bay Area, then fly back to my everyday life in Las Vegas with my new plus-one. I had already dreamed up and birthed a business—my first honorary child, as I would so fondly say—before becoming Austin's mom. How much more life-changing could having a child be? While pregnant, I had already begun planning my birthday party in February, a ski trip to Colorado with my family and my newborn.

Reality didn't set in until a snowstorm hit Colorado and my aunt, the matriarch on my father's side of the family who lived in Denver, called to tell me there is no way I should bring a two-month-old baby to Colorado. That was the moment I realized life as I knew it had completely changed, and my new normal would be that this little person would now be at the center of my every life decision. It was truly no longer all about me.

He was delivered by this petite Southeast Asian female doctor, and his pediatrician was a woman of color too. Between me, his grandmother, his godmother, and his doctors, by design and Divine intervention, all the women who shaped his life were women of color with significant professional roles. Austin has only known women in prominent positions. And his circle of male role models are also men of prominence. That was intentional; I wanted to make sure he was surrounded by great men, too. It was important to me that Austin saw men that look like him doing great things in life, as a way to inspire him.

For the first few weeks after giving birth to my son, I didn't sleep well because he was up every hour, and because, as a new mom, I was filled with anxiety. To make life easier for the both of us, I just had him sleep in bed with me, so I could nurse him and not have to get up all throughout the night. I remember being so tired all the time. I didn't feel like my full self until he was three years old.

Since I was able to work remote, I was home with my newborn son for seventeen months. Then he was off to daycare, which was good for him. He went to a wonderful daycare with a woman who'd reimagined her home into this fun, creative learning space. Although I enjoyed our bonding time for his first seventeen months, it was the right amount of time for both of us.

Now that all my decisions were based on what was best for my son, I would learn that I would also need to learn how to carve out some time just for me. It took seven years and the gift of my then-boss and mentor: professional coaching for one month with a coach (whom I still have, twenty years later). I learned the need for a balance of life. To achieve balance as a single mom and working professional, I had to start carving out time for myself, at least a couple hours a week. Time for me and just me to do something fun and playful for peace of mind, and quality time to love on me. I learned how to do this through a fun, creative book titled *The Artist's Way*.[3] *The Artist's Way* is a self-help book that guides readers to unlock their creativity through fun, transformative exercises.

What I learned from these things helped me to create the 12 New Things concept of "Shonda time," also known as "me time," my spin on *The Artist's Way*'s "artist date." On my "Shonda time" excursions, I challenge and encourage myself to discover New Things to do on the day and time I have carved out just for me. Many people know how busy my work schedule is as a business owner working on multiple mega-projects and wonder how I do it all. My first answer is prayer, and the second is the 12 New Things Lifestyle. Both require faith. And the latter gives me the splash of fun needed for balance.

Now, caring for my aging parents was not a responsibility I intentionally volunteered to take on. It was a natural progression that came with them being part of the village that helped me raise and surround my son with love. As my son aged, so did they, and I was near to support. This

---

3   Julia Cameron, *The Artist's Way: A Spiritual Path to Higher Creativity* (New York: Tarcher/Putnam, 1992).

was definitely a New Thing for me. I never thought I would have my father live with me for close to thirty years, and at one point, my mother too! The story of them living with me even led to another New Thing: the first original script my brother and I wrote. It's a sitcom—the most hilarious story—about how I, a single mom, navigate living with two young-at-heart, aging parents.

Although the journey is not how I had planned it, it has been filled with gratitude because my son was able to know his grandparents in a way I did not get to know mine. My father's parents were deceased by the time I was born, and my mother's parents lived in Houston, Texas, all of their lives. Grandparents to me were extended loved ones whom I saw once a year and were removed from my daily life. On the other hand, for my son, grandparents are like the best extended parent you could have, full of unconditional love and unlimited admiration! It is my son and parents' closeness that kept me in the Bay Area.

My parents have joined me on many 12 New Things adventures, such as camping in Yosemite as a family, Father's Day in the Bahamas, and even New Year's in Dubai. It is a joy for me to share these things with my parents, especially since they afforded me an incredible childhood full of international travel. It is the least I can do. As my parents age, I find myself having to be more in tune to things I had never considered, such as knowing where the local hospitals are when we travel. Bearing witness to my parents aging in the midst of raising my son into a man gave me an up-close look at how close in proximity these two cycles of life fall for the generation in the middle.

My parents have both committed to a 12 New Things Lifestyle, enjoying and experiencing New Things in their golden years. It is inspiring to watch them and their friends learn new sports, take new adventures, and travel to new places. It has been refreshing to watch my friends' parents learn new hobbies, such as gardening and golf, as part of their 12 New Things journeys.

As a parent, at some point you'll probably find yourself in a home with many generations under one roof, whether it's just during the holidays when everyone gathers or it's for decades, as it was for me. When one or both elderly parents move in or grown children move back home, your new situation needs understanding and boundaries on all sides. Everyone must be aware of each other's expectations and of what is needed to run the home. Everyone must do their part to keep the peace and unity. Everything from sit-down family dinners prepared by one or more on specific nights to everyone planning and taking a 12 New Things family vacation can generate a healthy, happy atmosphere. It's also helpful if each person's role and responsibilities in the household are made clear. Simply breaking down chores can make it so one person doesn't end up overburdened and resentful.

My mom has always worked and loved to work, and she always took care of our home. She is the best at making everyone around her feel special. I do not recall this story, but my aunt, who lived with us while she was in college, recalls my mom working, coming home to prepare dinner, and not serving dinner until my dad came home from work. I do remember us all eating dinner together until I was a junior in high school. I think that was about the time my mom stopped cooking every night and started doing it only on Sundays. This was fine with me because around this time, I began driving and ordering takeout Chinese food every day when I was not on a diet. The point is, members of the family need to communicate about how they want to contribute to the running of the household, and these conversations can change over time.

My mom enjoys working and cooking, so it never seemed like a burden for her to do both. All of my friends in two-parent households and all my married aunts worked and took care of the home too. Now, my mother did draw the line in one area. When my brother and I were in elementary school, my mother hired a housekeeper/nanny named Ana. Ana was a middle-aged woman originally from Hungary who remained in our lives from the time I was ten years old until I graduated from college.

As the older children move on to have their own lives, it's important to keep communication going, plan family time, and do things together. On the other hand, we need to allow space for adult children to learn and experience their own New Things.

The 12 New Things Lifestyle can help with the family dynamic in any variety of family situations. No matter how your particular family unit is made up, 12 New Things can help you to give everyone an outlet to do New Things to take family members out of their comfort zones, enhance their lives, and renew their spirits. It can also be a prompt for you to both take time for yourself and to support your partner or primary caregiver so everyone comes home as the best, fullest, ever-growing version of themselves.

EXERCISES:

1. As a family, whether or not you live together, plan a trip to somewhere none of you have gone before. Pick someplace that will have activities for everyone to do together and that everyone is excited about.

2. Plan a family visit to a local event, museum, or activity you have all thought about but not taken time to do. Don't forget to include any significant other people in your adult child's or elder parent's life they would like the family to begin to know. If

you're looking to start an activity to share regularly as a family, think of hobbies that are accessible and beneficial for everyone. You can start your search online, at the local hobby store, or see what your city's recreational facilities have to offer.

3. Seniors: No age should deter your senior parents from trying something new. Have them make a list of New Things they have never attempted but would like to try. From new hobbies to travel, encourage them to do one of those New Things each month.

4. Children: Help your children to plan age-appropriate New Things each month. Do something new each month with your children, like discovering new places in your hometown or trying a new food.

5. Adult Children: No matter how old your adult children are, tell them about your adventures in the 12 New Things Lifestyle and encourage them to pursue their own New Things.

"Honor your father and your mother, so that you may live long in the land the Lord, Lord your God has given you."

—Exodus 20:12

IN A NUTSHELL

Dear 12 New Things Adventurers,

In closing, it's a lifestyle! I have truly had fun reminiscing and sharing my personal experiences with you. My hope is that by hearing about my adventures, you are inspired to begin your own 12 New Things journey today, tomorrow, or at whatever big or small mile-marker you choose. (If your birthday is around the corner, that is always a fun time to start!) Open your mind to exploring and experiencing 12 New Things to uplift, encourage, and motivate you to do better throughout the next twelve months. Find the 12 New Things that will open your mind, body, and spirit to new experiences and connect with new people.

Remember: You're never too old; as long as you live, there can always be time to find New Things to learn, enjoy, and improve yourself. You can always find a way to accomplish your New Thing.

But don't delay! There's no time like the present. It's time to begin planning the 12 New Things Lifestyle to do new and different things to move you out of your comfort zone. Use the stories in this book to guide you into trying something new and different each month for a year. Don't worry; I'm here to get you started!

Getting organized is definitely the first step on the 12 New Things journey. Pull together the tools you will need to plan and execute your New Things. Look at what you already have available to you in your space. Then, head to the office supply store to find other items to help your creativity flow.

1. Journal

Journals are available in many styles and sizes. Find one with a layout and look that inspires you and makes you want to fill its pages. Some have dated pages or places to write the date and title for each entry. Some include a ribbon to mark your spot, somewhere to put your pen, or pockets to store other spare pages. Some have spiritual or positive messages of inspiration to help you reach your daily goal. Pick a journal that means something to you and that fits your lifestyle.

2. Calendar

You will need a calendar that includes all of the holidays. It should be large enough to add your important personal dates throughout the year. There are no rules here—select the type of calendar that works best for you. It could be a calendar on the wall, in a binder, the size to pop into your purse or backpack, or the one on your cell phone. You just need to have one with you to assist in planning your year.

3. Your Vision Board

Next, look for a corkboard, a whiteboard, a pinboard, or a presentation board. Once you know the type of vision board you want to create, collect magnets, pins, markers, tape, or stickies so you can start decorating the board. Once you have identified your dream adventure, you will use the board to picture it in detail using cutouts from travel magazines, printed images from the internet, or photos of the type of place, vacation, or adventure you want to envision.

―――

Once you have everything together, find a place to post your vision board and a place to keep your journal and calendar, if you use physical ones. This will be your cozy creative space to have your morning beverage and be free to dream. Write in your journal each morning, updating your list from the day before and looking ahead to what exciting New Things you have coming up.

It is essential to maintain a daily ritual that inspires you to keep doing New Things. Whichever type of calendar you use, this should be the place to organize yourself and mark down plans for future New Things. Studies have shown that just writing something down on paper greatly increases the likelihood that you'll get it done. If you use a phone calendar, be sure to set alerts to remind yourself of not just your daily to-do items but exciting adventures you have coming up. That extra reminder will get you excited to try these New Things.

Begin your first journaling session by spending some quality time with yourself. Take this opportunity to dream and reflect:

1. Write about your dreams of what you want to do, what you want to achieve in the next year, what places you want to visit, and what changes you want to see in your life.

2. Write a list of New Things you have never done that interest you.

3. Pick your first New Thing. It doesn't have to be huge. Research, plan, and create your checklist of the steps you'll need to take to do the New Thing.

I hope you realize that by opening yourself to New Things and pursuing adventure, you'll create a life that is enriched and fulfilled no matter how many times you have traveled around the sun. There is strength and growth in every New Thing you do and every change you make, no matter how big or small. Begin now: Embrace each New Thing with newfound courage to train yourself to pivot from a place of fear to one of joy, excitement, and enrichment.

Thank you so much for joining me on this 12 New Things journey. I look forward to hearing about your adventures and the personal growth found through your 12 New Things experience.

ACKNOWLEDGMENTS

I am forever grateful to the Lord Jesus Christ for the beautiful family I have been blessed with on both sides. My maternal and paternal families have the same morals, values, and joyful love. I am grateful for the best "twin" brother, collaborator, and co-creator I could ever ask for. Kente is more than a brother. He is my first lifelong friend, creative partner, and the one who blessed me with my only biological niece, the lovely Tyler Khimani. And my amazing uncles (Johnny, P.M., Warren, A.D., and Don), incredible aunts (Nancelia, Billie Ruth, Annette, and Maggie Vernece), and cousins who are more like nieces, nephews, and even siblings (love you, Moses-Sisters, Von and Shon). And to my godbabies, love you to the moon and back.

In addition to my beautiful family, I am grateful for the circle of friends I am blessed to have in my life, some for decades. Special thanks to my son's godparents, whom I love unconditionally: Maya and Tony, Shane and Zizzare. During various points in my life, you have been the shoulders that lifted me up, filling me with the love I needed—thank you! And an extra special note to Maya, who has been my longest sister-friend and trusted confidante: We have shared so many special moments; love and thank you. Rachelle and Ella, thank you for your friendship from childhood to adulthood and the years of love and laughter.

They say it takes a village to raise a child. It also takes a village to help you elevate your experience and soar in life. My village is composed of remarkable men and women, trusted advisors who poured love and support into me. I appreciate you and all your insights.

I want to acknowledge and thank Steven Kay, Esq., all my wonderful clients, joint venture partners, mentors and coaches, and one of the best collaborators, CeCe. To the most incredible team, #Team360, who have helped me expand my dream—it warms my heart to know I had a hand in helping you to achieve your dreams too—thank you! Special recognitions to Shonnell and Ramasses, my first two hires to Team 360 and most tenured team members; watching you both blossom into great leaders has been a blessing to behold. Which brings me to you, my dear 12 New Things community: You are also part of this village, and your support has been invaluable.

Thank you to my prayer warriors who have interceded for and prayed with me: Pastors Scurry, Pastors Carey and family, Dr. Tucker, and so many others.

ACKNOWLEDGMENTS

Dr. DeWitt, thank you—one conversation with you ignited and encouraged the light that lit the fire to bring the 12 New Things brand to life.

With love,

Photo by James Cant

ABOUT THE AUTHOR

Visionary | CEO | Author
Journalist | World Traveler

SHONDA SCOTT is an entrepreneur and visionary committed to change as a catalyst for personal and professional growth. Often identified as a self-made businesswoman, Shonda calls herself God-made, remaining rooted in her strong sense of faith. As the founder and CEO of 360 Total Concept, a management consulting firm, Shonda has led transformative projects with major organizations, municipalities, and key transit agencies. Under her leadership, over $200 million has been reinvested into underserved communities, fueling economic development and empowering small businesses.

Her entrepreneurial success and leadership have earned Shonda national recognition as an influential civic leader, advocate, and strategist. Shonda is also frequently featured as an expert on leadership, personal development, and innovation in media outlets and public forums.

Shonda's influence extends beyond business into politics, where her leadership and faith have earned national recognition. She has served as a presidential appointee under three United States presidents, and in 2023, the Presidential Lifetime Achievement Award, signed by President Biden and Vice President Harris, honored her for outstanding community service. Shonda was also inducted into Alameda County's Women's Hall of Fame for her contributions to business and community. In recognition of her dedication to humanitarian efforts, Shonda was awarded an Honorary Doctorate of Philosophy in Humanitarianism in 2023 from Leaders Esteem Christian Bible University.

A sought-after speaker and thought leader, Shonda shares her expertise in community development, economic empowerment, and transformational leadership across various industries.

As the executive producer and host of the popular talk show *Spotlight with Shonda Scott*, she continues to amplify the voices of national influencers and unsung heroes. The show is a platform where leaders, creators, and change-makers from various fields share their experiences, challenges, and advice for personal and professional success.

Her most personal initiative, the 12 New Things® challenge, began in 2019 as a self-improvement journey to try something new every month. What started as a personal resolution evolved into a nationwide movement, encouraging others to embrace change and unlock growth through new experiences. The 12 New Things Lifestyle has earned Shonda features in major publications, television segments, and op-eds, recognizing its profound impact on both personal and professional development.

A dedicated traveler, Shonda has visited over forty states and twenty-five countries, broadening her perspective on cultural diversity and community-building. Whether attending a women's conference in Mexico, exploring local Oakland spots, or hosting international retreats, she finds joy in every new experience.

Shonda's story is one of resilience, empowerment, and a commitment to lifting others through her message: Embrace change, challenge yourself, and never stop growing.

To learn more about Shonda Scott's work, speaking engagements, initiatives, and all things 12 New Things, visit 12newthings.com.